How to Listen to Jazz

HOW TO LISTEN TO JAZZ

— Ted Gioia —

BASIC BOOKS
A Member of the Perseus Books Group
New York

Published by Basic Books,
A Member of the Perseus Books Group

Books published by Basic Books are available at special discounts for bulk
purchases in the United States by corporations, institutions, and other
organizations. For more information, please contact the Special Markets
Department at the Perseus Books Group, 2300 Chestnut Street, Suite 200,
Philadelphia, PA 19103, or call (800) 810-4145, ext. 5000,
or e-mail special.markets@perseusbooks.com.

Library of Congress Cataloging-in-Publication Data

Names: Gioia, Ted.
Title: How to listen to jazz / Ted Gioia.
Description: New York : Basic Books, [2016] | Includes bibliographical
references and index.
Identifiers: LCCN 2016000587 | ISBN 9780465060894 (hardcover)
Subjects: LCSH: Jazz—Analysis, appreciation.
Classification: LCC ML3506 .G55 2016 | DDC 781.65/117—dc23
LC record available at http://lccn.loc.gov/2016000587

10 9 8 7 6 5 4 3 2 1

For my brother Dana, *il miglior fabbro*

"Listening is the most important thing in music."

—Duke Ellington

Contents

Introduction

What could be more mysterious than a work of music? When aliens arrive from their distant galaxy, they won't have much trouble understanding our food, sex, and politics—those all make perfect sense. But they will scratch their green scaly heads at why people plug music into their ears or get up and dance when the band starts to play. *Captain, we are unable to decipher the messages hidden in these three-minute bursts of sound, and the earthlings refuse to give us the code.* The sci-fi movies have it all wrong: extraterrestrials won't waste time blowing up the Eiffel Tower and the White House. They will be too busy trying to figure out the significance of a Bach fugue, the rituals of the electronic dance music scene, and the rules of jazz improvisation.

And that jazz performance may puzzle them most of all. What could be stranger than a band playing the *identical* song, night after night, but making it *different* each time? How do you crack that code? How do you pinpoint the epicenter of the elusive quality known as *swing*, praised so

lavishly by jazz fans but so resistant to explication or measurement? How do you grasp the structure of an idiom in
which so much seems spontaneous, made up on the spot,
and performed with headlong passion, yet is obviously
driven by rock-solid ground rules and shaped by revered
traditions? Above all, how do you penetrate the essence of
a practice so imponderable that, when jazz icon Fats Waller
was asked to define it, he allegedly warned, "If you have to
ask, don't mess with it."[1]

Yet there's something almost as mysterious as jazz:
namely, jazz critics. Who are these expert listeners, empowered to translate strange and wonderful sounds into a verbal
description, assign a score or grade—*this hot new record gets
four stars!*—and then move on to the next song? Music, by
definition, begins where linguistic meaning stops, yet these
critics earn their living by breaching the boundary, reducing melodies to words, and somehow convincing the rest
of us to give credence to their judgments. Aliens will certainly kidnap a few of these critics, plug them into the truth
machine, and force them to explain the secret meanings of
human music-making.

Of course, many earthlings are equally puzzled by critics. Where *do* those stars and scores come from? And the
critics don't add to their credibility by their antics. Those
well-known movie reviewers who decided to compress
their erudite assessments into a hand gesture—thumbs up
or thumbs down, like spectators at a gladiator show—didn't

do themselves or their profession any favors. Is it really that easy to be a critic? And what conclusion do we reach when we see one critic offer the thumbs up and the other give the thumbs down? If reviewing had any objective standards, and wasn't mere whim and opinion, wouldn't they agree most of the time?

The general public also holds a deep-seated suspicion, not entirely without justification, that the 'serious' critics despise precisely those works of art that most people love. Box-office hits, best sellers, chart-topping singles—they all are treated with scorn by these elitists, who then turn around and praise to the hilt some esoteric work no reasonable person would ever enjoy. Readers are often left wondering whether the authors aren't simply trying to impress them with their hipness or faux sophistication, rather than offer an honest appraisal of the work at hand.

Critics add to this distrust by making their process seem opaque and mysterious. They are very quick to give a ranking to a work, assigning stars or scores or thumbs, but rarely tell us how these scales are constructed or what priorities are involved in their application. Music magazines publish countless reviews touting four- and five-star albums, and dismissing the inferior two- and three-star alternatives, but where do we find an in-depth description of the ranking system itself? What values do these rankings embody? What assumptions are built into the scores and rankings? If music fans probe deeper into the process, they encounter lots of specifics about individual recordings but almost nothing about how critical judgments are formed.

Even though I have worked for many years as a critic, I still know what it's like to be a novice puzzled by the arcane aspects of the reviewer's craft. In my mid-thirties, I lived in Napa for a year, and in order to have intelligent conversations with my neighbors—almost all of them worked in the wine industry—I decided to improve my knowledge of grapes and vintages. This was a pleasant field of study, but I took it seriously and even shelled out some hard-earned cash to subscribe to a pricey newsletter by the influential wine connoisseur Robert Parker. Much to my surprise, I learned not only about wine but also some new twists on criticism. The sheer variety of ways he could describe the taste of a wine was stunning. *With mouthwatering black and blue fruits distinctly tinged by fruit pits, smoked meat, chalk, and a medicinal iodine note, this formidably concentrated wine never forgets its duty to refresh.* I could read a hundred or more of his short assessments of vintages at a sitting, and would soon forget about the wines, so lost was I in admiration of the many ways Parker had found to capture their ineffable qualities in words. How many ways can you describe the flavor of fermented grape juice? Parker never seemed to exhaust the possibilities, and at his best his descriptions possessed a certain wry poetry and metaphorical insight. I was writing a book on the history of jazz during that time in Napa, and I am convinced to this day that my own ability to describe music was improved by this immersion in wine culture and criticism.

Yet even after months of reading Parker's newsletter, I still couldn't explain the difference between a wine he assigned eighty-five points and another vintage that rated ninety-five. I enjoyed his prose, and even more I enjoyed the wines. But though I tasted the vintages, and concurred that he had guided me to many an outstanding bottle, I could only vaguely grasp what kinds of finely calibrated standards he had applied before writing the few sentences he used to describe them.

Yet as I look back on my own writings on music—which could now fill a shelf—I realize that I am just as guilty as Robert Parker and the thumbs-up-and-down movie critics. I've offered both praise and put-downs to many an artist over the years, but I've never actually outlined in detail the standards I apply in making these evaluations. I've sometimes made a few general comments on my process, but hardly with the degree of specificity the subject deserves.

And I'm not the only one. I've read hundreds of books on jazz, but I can't recall any critic actually explaining, at a detailed and granular level, what they were listening *for*. Sure, they talk about musicians and albums, and techniques and styles, but do they ever really invite readers inside the head of a critic (a scary thought!) and allow them to watch along as the evidence is sifted and assessments and decisions are made?

With that in mind, I've tried to lay bare my own process of listening in the pages ahead. I do this not just as a personal confession, or even as a guide to music appreciation—although both of those purposes are served—but also because this kind of close listening is the source of my pleasure as a consumer of music. My hope is that your enjoyment will also be deepened by these same listening strategies. Later we will move on to look at the structure and styles of jazz, and explore the leading practitioners of the idiom, but all this presupposes that we have some consensus on what we are trying to hear in this body of work. Listening is the foundation; everything else builds out of this starting point. Certainly some of what follows is subjective, but my hope is that you will walk away with a realization that this kind of deep critical listening and judgment is built on more than just personal taste, but draws on clear standards *inherent in the music itself* and how it has evolved. The music itself makes certain demands on the listeners, and the critic who articulates these demands has left subjectivity behind, at least to some degree.

You may come to disagree with some of the assessments and suggestions laid out here—and, in truth, all rules (my own included) have exceptions—but in even that instance, the process of grappling with them may serve to open your ears and expand your horizons. In any event, the views shared below were hard earned, things I grasped only after years or decades of studying the music. My hope is that by putting them down in writing I will help you enter more deeply into the mysterious process of 'appreciating' jazz.

ONE

The Mystery of Rhythm

L ET ME START WITH A PARABLE.
  A young scholar decides to devote his life to the study
of African rhythms. He moves to Ghana, where he learns
under the tutelage of more than a dozen master drummers.
He eventually spends a full decade immersed in the musical
traditions and practices of the region, but he supplements
these teachings with other sources of learning, whether in
the halls of Yale University or in the traditional communi-
ties of Haiti and other destinations of the African diaspora.
With each passing year, his expertise grows, and eventually
he becomes much more than a scholar. He is a full-fledged
practitioner who now carries on the tradition himself.

But when our expert returns to the United States, he
finds it difficult to convey the essence of these practices to
outsiders. He tries to teach students how to play the Da-
gomba drums, and they ask him the simplest question of all:

"How do I know when to enter? When do I start playing?" In Western music, there is an easy answer. The conductor waves a baton, or a bandleader counts off the beat, or the musical score provides a cue. But entering into the ongoing flow of a West African musical performance is a much different matter.

"I found that if I tried to demonstrate how to enter with one drum by counting from another drum's beat, I could not do it," our scholar admits in frustration. No amount of analysis or rule-making solves his problem. Finally, he realizes that the obstacle can be overcome only by moving away from analysis and entering into the realm of feeling. "The only way to begin correctly," he eventually discovers, "was to listen a moment and then start right in."[1]

Listen a moment and then start right in. There has to be more, no? A decade of apprenticeship, and this is the take-away? Yet this was the solution, beguiling in its apparent simplicity.

For those who devote the better part of a lifetime to the study of music, stories like this one are humbling. They testify to a magical element in the music, especially in its rhythmic essence, that eludes intellectualization. This aspect of the music must be felt, and if it isn't felt, academic dissection is futile. The scholar must become more than a scholar to grasp it, and the student determined to follow on the same path must be willing to leave pedagogy behind and embrace something so elusive that, at times, it can hardly be described.

But all parables come with an implicit lesson, and there is one in this story. Our tale—a story from the real life of John Miller Chernoff, one of the most discerning experts on African rhythm and drumming—testifies to the power of *listening*. In our parable, hearing trumps analysis. And if this superiority of the ear over the brain humbles the trained musicologist, it also should give a dose of encouragement to the outsider who doesn't know the terminology and codified procedures of the aural arts. Listening, not jargon, is the path into the heart of music. And if we listen at a deep enough level, we enter into the magic of the song—no degrees or formal credentials required.

This book is built on the notion that careful listening can demystify virtually all of the intricacies and marvels of jazz. This is not to demean the benefits of formal music study or classroom learning. Yet we do well to remember that the people who first gave us jazz did so without much formal study—and, in some instances, with none at all. But they knew how to *listen*. And, like Chernoff and his students, they learned to use that capacity as a touchstone in unlocking their own creative potential.

In a similar manner, we do well to recall that the African musical traditions at the root of jazz rarely distinguished between performers and audiences. All members of the community participated in its musical life. Those raised in these cultures would reject the notion that special training or skills might be required to join in the exhilaration and excitement of music-making. In this tradition, there are no outsiders. Everyone has the capability to grasp the music at its most essential level. But there is one inescapable requirement: they must listen, and listen deeply.

These considerations are important in assessing all aspects of jazz, but especially when dealing with its quasi-magical rhythmic essence. Science has expanded considerably our knowledge of the properties of rhythm in recent decades. We can now isolate and measure the impact of rhythm on our brainwaves, our hormones, our immune system, and other aspects of our physiology.[2] But these studies have only deepened the mystery. Why does our body respond so powerfully to the beat? Why don't dogs, for example, match their body movements to external rhythms? Why don't chimpanzees or cats or horses dance to the beat? They don't, and you can't train them to do so. Yet every human society and community provides an outlet for this irresistible response to rhythm—sometimes even relying on it as a pathway to the divine. This propensity is hardwired into our bodies, perhaps into our souls, but do we even know where to start in assessing its aesthetic dimensions?

So here, at the very outset of this book, we run into a huge problem. We need to start with the first and most important ingredient in jazz, its ecstatic rhythmic quality. This is the most difficult aspect of the music to circumscribe and almost impossible to convey in words. Yet if you learn how to listen deeply to this aspect of jazz, you will have made a huge step toward grasping the essentials of the music. So let's try to unlock the mystery of jazz rhythm. To do that I need to lay bare my own approach to hearing the beat and share the techniques and attitudes that have helped me in my own attempts to penetrate its magic.

The Pulse (or Swing) of Jazz

The first thing I listen for is the degree of rhythmic cohesion between the different musicians in the band. Some jazz critics might describe this as *swing*. Certainly that's part of it, at least in most jazz performances. But there is something more than mere finger-tapping momentum involved here. In the great jazz bands, you can hear the individual members lock together rhythmically in a pleasing way that involves an uncanny degree of give-and-take, but with a kind of quirkiness that resists specific definition. If you listen to the most innovative rhythm sections—for example, the Count Basie band from the prewar years, the Bill Evans trio from the early 1960s, the Miles Davis and John Coltrane groups from the mid-1960s, or ensembles led by Vijay Iyer, Brad Mehldau, and Jason Moran in the current day—you hear a paradoxical type of cooperation taking place in real time. The musicians are adapting to each other but also insisting on their own prerogatives. They are somehow accommodating and demanding at the same time. This pleasing give-and-take results in a holistic synergy that emerges from the blending of individual personalities. The pulse of the music feels alive and potent.

At the other extreme, you can hear amateur bands struggling to achieve this same degree of effortless cohesion. And you can perhaps learn more about swing from listening to the bands that fail to achieve it. Frequently in the pages ahead, I will advise you to seek out and listen to lesser-skilled musicians. You are probably skeptical, and I can hardly blame you. Has any music appreciation teacher ever focused on inferior performances? But I'm convinced that only by listening long and hard to second-rate performers will you ever really appreciate what the world-class artists have achieved. Fortunately this is easy to do nowadays— just go to YouTube and do a search on "student jazz band." If you listen to a dozen or so beginning and intermediate bands, you will grasp the gap between them and the top-notch professional ensembles. The single biggest limitation of these groups is the awkwardness with which they blend together. You can hear the tension in their playing. You can feel viscerally the sluggishness in their swing. Like a car that needs a tune-up, they aren't operating on all cylinders.

I don't say this with any malice. I've been there. I've lived through this entire struggle myself. Between the ages of fifteen and twenty-five, I spent more than ten thousand hours at the piano, and I know all the mistakes of novice jazz musicians—because I made *every one of them* myself. In fact, the harshest reviews I've ever delivered as a music critic have been directed at myself. I made a number of recordings of my performances in my late teens and early twenties, and later I *destroyed all of them*. As I subsequently explained my reasons to a curious inquirer: "My musical phrases were fine, except for how they began and how they ended, and everything that came between." My fingers were dexterous, and I took some pride in my tone control, but many of the most fundamental aspects of musicality came only after much consternation and struggle. Even thinking about this period in my musical education is painful for me nowadays.

I sometimes wish that my accumulated learning had come easier. I've spent enough time around musicians with amazing ears and instincts to envy the ease with which they assimilate the jazz craft. When I had the opportunity to play with Stan Getz, I could tell that he instantly heard everything that was happening on the bandstand. If I put an altered note into a chord, he immediately reacted to it. I remember him coming up to me once after we had played "You Stepped Out of a Dream" and commenting: "I liked the way you slipped in that augmented chord." The fact °that he referred to the harmony with that degree of specificity was rare for Getz—it sometimes seemed to me that he still dealt in a pure world of sounds while the rest of us were caught up in our harmonic rules and terminology. But even if I was surprised by the analytical attitude in his comment, I wasn't at all shocked at his close attention to a very casual and brief substitute chord I had inserted, which had lasted no more than a second or two in the song. Getz's ears were, in my opinion, one-in-a-million, and I had spent enough time with him to realize that nothing could happen in a performance that would leave him unprepared. He would respond, and without any need to consider harmonic rules and scale patterns.

I wasn't like that. I have a good ear. Some people might even say I have an outstanding ear. I participated in a study years ago in which my ability to hear and identify intervals was measured, and the researchers told me I was faster at this than anyone they had tested. But I still know that a sizable gap exists between me and someone like Stan Getz or Chet Baker, people who hear everything and don't even have to think about it. They have a biological advantage, plain and simple. I had to draw on different strengths, analytical and methodological skills that I have honed over the years, and I was fortunate that they proved their own value in the long run. But the bottom line is that I learned the jazz craft a day at a time, with much effort expended in the process.

Sometimes I think I became a better teacher and critic because I had to be detailed and systematic in my own learning. Someone once pointed out to me that the best NBA coaches—people such as Phil Jackson, Pat Riley, Gregg Popovich—weren't the most gifted players. When I was a youngster, I saw both Riley and Jackson play, and I can attest that they spent most of the game on the bench. But the very fact that they had to fight for playing time, and work more tenaciously than their colleagues, gave them hard-earned insights that the natural-born geniuses never have to worry about. I feel the same about my own development as a musician. I learned slowly and carefully, and when (as I will often do in this book) I call attention to the ways an amateurish musician falls short, rest assured that I make this comparison with sympathy and a dose of self-recognition.

But let's get back to swing (or, in this case, the *absence* of swing). This lack of rhythmic cohesion can be easily heard in second-rate jazz bands. And even listeners who don't know much about music will sense it subliminally. They won't get the same kind of satisfaction and enjoyment from the performance. And this is not just the case in fast, finger-snappin' numbers, but even in meditative mood pieces and romantic ballads where the term "swing" perhaps doesn't do justice to the rhythmic character of the music. You may think you know nothing about jazz, but if you take the time to compare amateur and professional bands, you will find that you can soon tell the difference from their varying levels of comfort and confidence in their rhythmic interaction.

Let's now forget about those awkward student bands and turn our attention to the masters of the music. After listening to an amateur ensemble, check out a group of top-tier professionals playing the same song, and marvel at the difference. Can we pinpoint the essence of swing in the music of the premier jazz bands? One way of doing this is to listen to the same performance repeatedly and focus on different instruments with each repetition. If you are seeking out the secret source of swing, a good place to start is with the locking together of the bass and drums. This may be the single most satisfying sound in all of jazz, at least when it's done by premier artists. Check out how bassist Paul Chambers interacts with drummer Philly Joe Jones on those classic jazz recordings from the 1950s; or Ron Carter and Tony Williams in the 1960s; or Christian McBride and Brian Blade in the current day. No, they aren't household names—bassists and drummers are rarely the leaders of jazz ensembles—but the stars wouldn't shine quite so brightly if these partners at the back of the bandstand didn't possess such powerful musical chemistry.

This mysterious factor in a performance is hardly re-stricted to jazz. The 'secret sauce' behind many successful popular songs is the degree of cohesion between the indi-vidual musicians, the effortless blending of each individual's personal sense of time into a persuasive holistic sound. It's hardly a coincidence that the most admired accompanists in the record industry have almost always come in teams. Musicians speak with rapt admiration about the Wrecking Crew or the Funk Brothers or the Muscle Shoals Sound—these names refer to teams of studio musicians, rarely stars themselves, but key participants on countless hit records. Producers kept hiring them because they realized that this well-honed collective interaction was just as important as a big-name superstar in turning tracks into hits. The best jazz bands are no different. Even though jazz is a highly individualistic art form, and its leading practitioners are dis-cussed in quasi-heroic terms, this crucial ingredient—my starting point in evaluating a performance—transcends the personal and resides in the collective.

As mentioned above, it's hard to define what goes into this effortless swing, but we can identify, with some specificity, what doesn't. First of all, the pleasing pulse of a world-class jazz band has almost nothing to do with rhythmic precision or keeping a steady tempo. If that were true, a software-driven beat would be superior to a jazz drummer, and that is hardly the case. Like John Henry in the famous folk ballad, jazz musicians beat machines, and the competition isn't even close. By the way, I am not overly concerned if a jazz band gradually changes its tempo during a song—although my experience tells me that acceleration is more acceptable to the listener than deceleration. If you pick up speed as you go along, the listeners may even find it exhilarating, but slowing down is usually painful to hear. Yet, in either case, the secret of the jazz beat cannot be measured with a metronome.

Some years ago I worked with an expert in computer analysis of rhythms, and together we tried to understand what was actually happening to the beat in music that possessed a strong sense of swing.[3] What we learned was that especially exciting performances tended to break the rules. Notes were not played right on top of the beat but in a variety of places in the continuum of rhythm, and sometimes they were employed in ambiguous ways. Some melodic phrases seemed to linger between a duple and a triple subdivision of the rhythm, and this ability to exist between the strictly delineated pulsations of traditional Western music is probably one of the key reasons for the appeal of jazz and other idioms that draw on African roots. You can't read this kind of music off the page—for the simple reason that traditional Western systems of notation can't contain it—but a listener can feel it, and a skilled jazz player can create it spontaneously.

Three specific kinds of songs provide an excellent measure of a jazz band's rhythmic cohesion. The first is perhaps the most obvious: Can the group handle a very fast tempo? As the pulsations move beyond three hundred beats per minute, and especially as they approach 350 beats per minute, the musicians face considerable challenges in simply staying together, let alone maintaining a sense of effortless swing. If you look back and trace the evolution of jazz, you will find that performers got much better at these breakneck tempos during the period from 1935 to 1950. Today's jazz musicians are, in many ways, better trained than their predecessors, especially in terms of assimilating techniques in a systematic and codified manner, but they are still tested at these warp speeds. Certainly jazz can't be reduced to a demonstration of rapid-fire technique. In fact, some improvisers have justifiable reasons for avoiding these tempos. I understand their hesitancy. Even under ideal conditions, it's hard to translate what you hear in your head to your instrument, and at ultrafast tempos musicians are tempted to rely on instincts and reflexes rather than real-time melodic improvisation. Even so, few things thrill me more than hearing a top-notch jazz group that can thrive at a blistering pace. And these tempos provide a useful barometer of jazz instrumental prowess.

But, believe it or not, a very slow number can actually be more difficult than a barn burner. If you listen to a wide range of groups playing jazz at around forty beats per minute, you will find that some can handle it without a problem, but in many instances you can hear the tension and discomfort in their playing. Perhaps one or more musicians in the band will even 'double up the beat' in response, playing clearly demarcated rhythmic patterns in between the pulses—not so much because they sound good, but because it's easier to hold the group together with these guideposts in between the beats. In some instances, the entire rhythm section doubles the rhythm: all of a sudden it sounds as if the tempo is twice as fast, and a ballad takes on a bouncy quality. I won't say this is always wrong; sometimes a bouncy ballad is just what the audience needs to hear. But when I am evaluating the band's skill level, I prefer to hear how the musicians handle the slower tempo. Does it breathe? Is it relaxed? Is it dreamy and ethereal? Or is it stiff and ungraceful? When the musicians sound much more comfortable after doubling the tempo (which is often the case), you can often discern—if only by comparison—how less skilled they were at the slower pulse.

But I have found that a third kind of song is perhaps an even better measure of a band's rhythmic cohesion. I've never heard anyone else mention this kind of piece as a litmus test of swing, but I'm convinced that it may be the single best gauge of a group's ability to work holistically as a jazz band. I am referring to a pulse just slightly faster than a typical human heartbeat. These kinds of songs operate in an awkward midpoint between slow and medium tempos—they are too fast to serve as dreamy ballads but too slow to treat as bouncy midtempo swingers. A song of this sort requires a very relaxed kind of delivery but also needs a clear source of propulsion. Many musicians are tempted to rush the beat, and the song thus ends up at an easier tempo to swing. Others are vigilant in keeping strict time, yet the performance sounds sluggish. But the best jazz bands operate comfortably at this pulse, and their playing sounds as effortless as breathing, nothing hurried or cut short. Listen to Count Basie's recording of "Li'l Darlin'" if you want to hear how this is done at a very high level of virtuosity. Of course, the irony here is that the music on this track hardly sounds difficult. But that's what it looks like to succeed at this game.

This may sound like a contradiction, but I listen for this same quality of relaxation even in the fastest tempos. This isn't a hard-and-fast rule—and on occasion I can enjoy a band that sounds as if it is almost out-of-control, operating on the verge of meltdown. But this is a tightrope act that few groups can consistently pull off. Very little space separates operating at the brink and falling into the abyss. The bands I have admired most for their up-tempo work—Art Blakey's Jazz Messengers and Oscar Peterson's trio come immediately to mind here—almost always seem in total command of the situation, regardless of the tempo. The music sounds fast, but never rushed or labored.

Here's a final tip on how to tell if a band is in synch. When a group is working together effectively, the individual musicians don't need to play so many notes. A soloist can toss off casual phrases, and each one seems to hit the mark. An accompanist can underplay, and the group still swings. On the other extreme—and I know this, once again, from painful personal experience—when the band's rhythmic cohesion is floundering, each individual in the group is tempted to overplay. This is almost a matter of instinct. It's no different from a second-rate basketball team: when they fail to operate together as a unit, individuals forget the plays, and everyone starts freelancing and going one-on-one. In a band as on the field of play, lots of activity is no substitute for skilled execution.

As you apply these listening strategies, you will find that you are gauging yourself as much as the music. When hearing jazz musicians whose rhythmic command is at the highest level, you will feel yourself drawn more deeply into the flow of the music. The performance will be more satisfying, more compelling. The confidence of the performers will translate itself into a visceral sense of rightness among the audience. This is more than a subjective response. Consider doing these listening sessions with others, and compare your assessments of the various jazz bands on your playlist. Score them on their rhythmic cohesiveness, their ability to enter into a flow state, and the mastery of their beat. You will almost certainly find that, as you get more experienced in listening, your rankings will converge with those of other skilled listeners. There will still be room for personal preferences in these evaluations. One fan might prefer hot and fast, another cool and relaxed—but both will be able to discern the difference between the greats and not-so greats. Once you have achieved this ability to 'feel' the rhythms, you will have made a huge leap in your capacity to understand and enjoy jazz.

TWO

Getting Inside the Music

EVEN IF I'M A MUSIC CRITIC AND HISTORIAN, I'M STILL NO DIFFERENT
from any other fan. I listen to music for pleasure, just
like everyone else. But unlike most people, I feel compelled
to analyze the music and try to pinpoint *why* I enjoy it.
What hidden factors distinguish a moving performance
from a blasé one? Why am I riveted by Billie Holiday and
Frank Sinatra, but when I go to a restaurant on karaoke
night, I ask to be seated as far from the music as possible?
The song might even be the same—Sinatra songs apparently come prepackaged with karaoke machines—but the
effect couldn't be more different.

When we turn to the experts for guidance on the
sources of our aural pleasures and phobias, we encounter a hopeless jumble. Over the last generation, academics
have tried to demystify aesthetic taste and show that it is a
social construct driven by constantly shifting cultural and

economic factors. Yet during this same period, neuroscientists, evolutionary biologists, cognitive psychologists, and
other researchers have adopted a diametrically opposed
position. They have produced stacks of research supporting the view that our responses to music and the other
arts are embedded in biological universals, inescapable and
ever-present in human society. Do these folks ever talk to
each other? They seem to work at the same universities, so
maybe someone can arrange a sit-down.

For my part, I've learned from both camps, but refuse to
give the last word to either. A major focus of my research,
especially during the last two decades, has been cross-
cultural convergences in the ways people sing and play musical instruments, and my work in this area has convinced
me that performance standards are hardly local and arbitrary. If you sing a lullaby, the baby is expected to fall asleep,
and this is true across national boundaries and generational
divides. When musicians play a dance number, they want
people to move their feet; that's true at an EDM concert
today, just as it was true in ancient societies. Every member
of the human species draws, to some extent, on a common
musical ethos. If that weren't the case, we wouldn't gather
together to enjoy shared musical experiences or be able to
discuss the matters addressed in this book. On the other
hand, I find that the neuroscientists and biologists often
overstate their claims and that colorful discussions about
"your brain on music" do little to enhance our appreciation
of any given work. As soon as they try to assess something

concrete and specific—for example, a Miles Davis solo or a Billie Holiday performance—the scientists offer few insights. The masterpiece will never be encompassed by neural analysis.

This is where music critics, those devilish folks who act as if they have all the answers, ought to fill the gap. They deliver the most value when they are able to navigate between these two extremes, avoiding the doctrinaire aspects of both sides—those who pretend that music is objective science and those who insist it is subjective whimsy—but drawing on the valid learnings of both camps. My way of balancing these tensions is by focusing on the music itself, rather than on my body chemistry or brainwaves and my careful listening tells me that we can learn the most about the magic of song by paying close attention to the basic building blocks of its construction. Put another way, music has its own chemistry, and sometimes we need to apply a microscope and peer into its atomic (or even subatomic) structures to grasp its impact on a macro level. Our subjective response is part of this analysis, but it is always just that, a *response*, and comes with a *responsibility*—a related word that conveys the meaning in the original Latin of *obligation*. This is how we ought to view the music critic's craft: the work in question imposes an obligation on these professional listeners, and they in turn must strive to live up to its demands.

The same is true of the casual fan who hopes to learn more about jazz. Let's see what happens when we try to expand our listening skills and grapple with this deep level of song. In the previous chapter, we looked at rhythm and swing. Let's now move to an even more granular level of scrutiny, and look inside the individual notes and phrases.

Phrasing

As noted in the previous chapter, the band's collective pulse—or perhaps I should call it the group's *metabolism*—is the first thing I listen for in a jazz performance, but the second, and just as important, is the way musicians shape their phrases. At this point, I start focusing more on the individual members of the group. Their skill at phrasing is especially evident in their improvised solos, but the superior jazz artist can stand out even when simply stating a melody or responding to the phrases of bandmates.

Listen, for example, to Johnny Hodges play "Come Sunday" on the recording of Duke Ellington's debut Carnegie Hall concert on January 23, 1943. He takes a full two minutes to play a thirty-two-bar melody. The written chart contains fewer than a hundred notes, and Hodges didn't write any of them; in fact, he probably only saw them for the first time a few days before he performed the music. Yet he plays the melody with such commitment and authority that you would think he was expressing his most deeply felt emotions on stage that night. I could say the same for John Coltrane's melody statement of "Lush Life," or Stan Getz's performances of "Blood Count," or any number of Miles

Davis ballads. Even before these artists start improvising, merely when they are interpreting a written melody, they demonstrate their mastery and express their individuality.

Some claim that there are no objective standards that can be applied to a jazz musician's phrasing. From this perspective, every improviser can choose how to construct improvised lines, and any outsider's attempt to distinguish good from bad is arbitrary. Have those who make these kinds of sweeping statements ever taught student musicians? Have they worked with young musicians and helped them develop over months and years, watching as they learn how to expand the range and depth of their improvised phrases— no different from an athlete working on strength and conditioning? Music teachers do this as a routine matter, and their mindset and ways of listening to a performance can serve as a touchstone for the critic or casual fan. Spend a day auditioning students for a jazz program, and you will no longer believe that all phrases are created equal.

At this rudimentary level of performance, the musicians tend to rely repeatedly on a small number of rhythmic patterns in their phrases. Even if the notes they play are different, the rhythmic structures of the phrases are often identical. Such improvisers might sound convincing for a single chorus, but if the solo goes on long enough, even novice listeners will perceive an inescapable monotony in the proceedings. Sometimes the phrases come across as boringly symmetrical, locked into two-bar or four-bar formulas that might sound okay in isolation but seem tired and unimaginative when repeated over and over again. In other instances, amateur improvisers betray their limitations by starting phrases on the same beats—for example, beat 1 of every other bar—time and time again. If you took away the rest of the band, and just listened to the soloist without accompaniment, you could still hear where the bar lines begin and end because they are telegraphed so obviously in the improvised phrases.

These kinds of limitations are all the more noticeable when heard in the current day, if only because professional jazz musicians have gotten much better over the passing decades at phrasing across the bars and structural demarcation points in the music. Back in the 1930s, when Coleman Hawkins started playing phrases that continued through the turnaround at the end of a chorus—that juncture at the conclusion of the song's form when almost any other horn player would have stopped for a breath—he signaled a major advance in how jazz musicians conceptualized their solos. Even earlier, in the 1920s, when Louis Armstrong played his extravagant introduction to "West End Blues" or navigated through the stop-time chorus on "Potato Head Blues," he was showing that jazz phrasing required more than just syncopation and swing but also an ability to impose the improviser's personal rhythmic sensibility on the composition. Lesser musicians, both then and now, sometimes sound as if it's the song that is playing them, rather than they who are playing the song. But with the master artist you never have any doubt who is in charge.

Let's marvel at Armstrong for a moment. We will return to him at several points in this book, but he demands our attention at this juncture. In the 1920s, he not only demonstrated the greatest mastery of jazz phrasing of any musician of his generation but literally invented countless syncopated phrases still used by improvisers all over the world. Armstrong is often praised for his famous tracks and live performances, but perhaps the most impressive testimony to his mastery of jazz phrasing came at a session almost completely forgotten by music historians. And for a good reason: the recordings were never issued, and are lost today—likely destroyed long ago. In 1927, a music publisher decided to capitalize on Armstrong's growing renown by releasing two books: *125 Jazz Breaks for Cornet* and *50 Hot Choruses for Cornet*. But Armstrong never actually wrote down any of this music. He simply showed up in a Chicago studio and improvised phrase after phrase after phrase into the horn of a primitive wax-cylinder recording device. The publisher hired songwriter Elmer Schoebel to transcribe these melodic lines, and though the original recordings have disappeared (and weren't even intended for release), the books survive. Method books don't usually rivet the attention of music fans, but these aren't your typical method books. They make clear that Armstrong simply had more jazz music in him, back during the Jazz Age, than any of his peers. He demonstrates endless ingenuity in constructing his breaks—two-bar phrases employed to impart momentum to an improvisation—and even after he has delivered fifty, a hundred, he still keeps coming up with more. The details of the recording session are lost to us, but it is likely that Armstrong did all this in just a few hours of studio time. That's what jazz genius looked like, circa 1927.

In subsequent decades, a host of other influential jazz artists worked to expand the rhythmic vocabulary of the music, and knowledgeable audience members now rightly expect to hear advanced melodic structures that are almost never encountered outside of jazz—fresh and unconstrained phrases far beyond anything occurring (with very few exceptions) in popular or even classical music. A lot of behind-the-scenes work goes into this kind of rhythmic mastery. And you can pursue some of these practice techniques yourself, even if you don't play an instrument. How? You start by tapping out different pulses with each hand—five-against-four, or four-against-three, and so on—making sure that each hand plays its pattern evenly and with perfect synchronization with the other. Then you take this practice a step further by adding a third rhythm with your left foot. And a fourth with your right foot.

Any volunteers to demonstrate this to the class?

I never get volunteers when I make this request. But are you surprised? Just imagine the challenge of pounding out four contrasting pulses simultaneously and keeping them all in time. Yet the most ambitious jazz musicians work on practice-room exercises of just this sort. The goal is to internalize the various rhythmic strategies to such a degree that they come out naturally and instinctively during performance. Phrases move effortlessly from one type of subdivision of the beat into another. In my own musical education, the moment of success came when I found I could play rhythmic patterns in the music that I could no longer analyze in real time. Put simply, I didn't know what I was doing at the piano. That may sound like a moment of failure to a classical musician, but from my perspective as an aspiring jazz improviser it signaled a breakthrough, an ability to fly above the ground beat. Of course, I could go back later and try to determine what I had done, and it would probably conform to some measurable way of splicing and dicing the phrases and bar lines. But at the moment of creation the music existed without reference to remembered rules and techniques.

This kind of flexibility in phrasing is one of the chief delights of hearing jazz music played by the masters of the idiom. And at the very highest level of jazz performance, I will subscribe to the above-cited view that there is no right or wrong way of phrasing. I am just as willing to admire a Bill Evans, who floats across the ground beat, as I am to praise a Thelonious Monk, who inserts disjunctive new rhythmic structures on top of the old ones. But the reality is that only a handful of jazz performers operate at this level, and that musicians not yet ready for the big time usually signal that fact by noticeable limitations in their vocabulary of phrases.

I listen for a number of other ingredients in phrasing. Above all, I like to hear a clear sense of what I call *intentionality* in a musician's phrasing. This is my term (stolen, I must admit, from the field of philosophy but used here in my own cranky way) for a musical phrase that reveals the total commitment of the improviser. After I have heard a phrase played with intentionality, I feel as if it is absolutely the only combination of notes that would have fit the circumstances. This doesn't mean it needs to be loud and boisterous—in fact, sometimes it can be a mere musical moan or whisper—but it possesses an ineffable rightness about it. In contrast, when I hear musicians playing practice-room patterns on the bandstand, or constructing facile phrases with their fingers that don't seem to involve their hearts and ears, I start to lose interest. The music conveys no strong sense of intentionality, perhaps even sounds rote.

Again, this may seem like a subjective judgment, but I believe this quality of intentionality is very much part of the music itself and not just a random response to it. You can especially hear it in how an improviser starts and ends a phrase. Dizzy Gillespie once claimed that the first thing that came into his mind when improvising was the rhythmic structure of the line, and only later would he choose the notes to play in the phrase. It sounds peculiar, but if you listen to Gillespie's best solos, every phrase has an authoritative quality—they start with a clear intentionality that lasts until the final note. In contrast, many lesser horn players seem to end their phrases when they run out of breath. This is the exact opposite of intentionality and sometimes conveys an impression, even with virtuosic performers, that they are struggling against the music.

For a useful exercise, listen to a range of jazz soloists, and evaluate the authority and confidence with which they begin and end their phrases. Mastery of this is much rarer than you might think. But listen to Lester Young or Miles Davis or Art Pepper or Chet Baker or Dizzy Gillespie or Wes Montgomery, and marvel at their skill in this facet of the improviser's art. You will sense their power at the starting point and finish line of their phrases, and you will also hear how this isn't a matter of loudness or energy, but rather a sense of clear intention and personal agency embodied in the melodic lines. Compare them with amateurs or lesser-skilled professionals, and you will hear the profound difference in how jazz musicians at various levels of proficiency construct their phrases.

I improved my ability to end a phrase by consciously imitating on the piano what Art Pepper did on the alto sax. (When stealing from other players, an older musician wisely advised me, choose a different instrument from your own, and people won't notice the theft.) But Dizzy Gillespie also captivated my imagination with his distinctive manner of constructing phrases, revealing incomparable skill at creating moments of climax and resolution in his melodic lines. His best work from the 1940s captures a visceral excitement that no one, in my opinion, has surpassed. Miles Davis, for his part, would never deliver that kind of Sturm und Drang but was incomparable at constructing oblique phrases, or perhaps I can even call them semi-phrases, given how few notes some of them contain. In Davis's best work, sounds move in and out of focus, and phrases stretch out or are compressed into mere murmurs or asides, yet they invariably possess the intentionality described above. For a musician, these role models serve as inexhaustible resources for learning and advancement in the jazz craft.

Of course, the best way to open up your ears to phrasing is by listening to the top tier of jazz vocalists. Hear how Billie Holiday lingers behind the beat, and achieves an almost conversational intimacy in her delivery. Check out how Frank Sinatra accents certain words, both to shape their meaning as well as to impart vitality to the melody line. Listen to Cassandra Wilson swoop down for those burnished low notes, or Cécile McLorin Salvant shift effortlessly from conversational tones to ethereal melody, or Tony Bennett enhance the emotional impact of a phrase with a slight thickening of tone at the proper moment. No one is better at these techniques than the jazz masters, and when I suggest you listen to them, it is partly for your musical education but also simply for your musical enjoyment.

Pitch and Timbre

When we listen to a jazz performance, we rarely focus on the specific tones. They go by so fast, who can really study them? In my musical education I was obsessed with hearing every little nuance in the music, but this proved far more difficult than I initially envisioned. When I was studying classical music, I could always turn to the written score. Here I could see each note and rest, every embellishment and dynamic marking, and all the harmonic ingredients laid out in black and white. But jazz musicians weren't quite so obliging. Their music flashed by at breathtaking speed, and I grabbed what my ears could, but that was akin to the proverbial act of drinking from a fire hose.

My breakthrough came in my late teens, when I acquired a turntable that had a setting for 17 revolutions per minute (rpm). Most people would have found this a useless option; albums and singles on the market were designed for playback at 33 and 45 rpm. But I found that if I spun an album at 17 rpm, it brought the song down an octave and slowed the music by half. Voilà! All of a sudden I could hear more clearly what was going on in a jazz performance. (You can slow down playback much more easily nowadays with software, but back then we all lived in an idyllic analog world.) Friends and family members probably thought I was crazy. Anyone coming into my bedroom would find me checking out Charlie Parker or Lester Young or Lee Konitz at half speed. Even jazz greats start to sound lugubrious, perhaps even a bit macabre, when heard in that manner. You wouldn't want to play this sluggish jazz for guests at a party. But given my needs, this super-slow jazz was a godsend. I could hear the individual notes with much more clarity and grasp many subtleties in the music that I might have missed otherwise. I felt like the referee who finally has access to a slow-motion replay and can now see the key details that went by too fast in real time. No one would want to watch a whole game in this manner, but at certain junctures in the action, the opportunity to go back and reexperience everything at a slower pace is invaluable.

I learned many things from this regimen of slow listening, but some of the most significant benefits came from grasping how much can happen even within the narrow confines of a single note. Of course, I already knew that jazz musicians took far more liberties with tone production than classical musicians, but now I heard this at a much deeper level. This distinctive aspect of the jazz trade has always been especially evident when listening to saxophonists.

The saxophone has never played a significant role in symphonic music, and when jazz musicians adopted the instrument in the 1920s and 1930s, there was no clear agreement on what constituted a 'correct' way of playing the horn. As a result, a wide range of approaches flourished, and jazz fans could pick their own favorite. Much debate took place over the relative merits of Coleman Hawkins's muscular and heavy tone versus Lester Young's light and fluid sound. Others might opt for Ben Webster's breathier and less insistent variant or, once we get to the 1940s, the astringent and penetrating alto attack of Charlie Parker.

Yet trumpeters also had their own distinctive ways of modifying the sound of their instrument, especially via the application of different mutes to the bell of their horn. If you listen to the pioneering players of brass instruments in jazz—for example, King Oliver's classic 1923 recordings or the early work of the Duke Ellington orchestra—you will see how important these sound colorings were to the power of the music. This kind of tone manipulation went far beyond anything heard in classical or marching band music and accounted for much of the excitement and popularity of the jazz idiom. The jazz cats played *dirty*, and fans loved precisely that quality in the music.

If you remember this simple fact, you will understand many developments in jazz that puzzle even serious fans. Many knowledgeable listeners are baffled by the success of the very first jazz recordings. These tracks, recorded by the Original Dixieland Jazz Band (ironically an all-white ensemble) in 1917, were huge sellers and played a decisive role in creating a commercial market nationwide for jazz music. But jazz fans who listen today to this band's early hits, such as "Livery Stable Blues" or "Tiger Rag," tend to dismiss them as corny novelty tunes—after all, the musicians actually resort to imitating animal sounds on their horns instead of delivery clean, crisp solos. How pathetic! And, true, nowadays we expect more from a jazz band than a whinny or a moo. But in the early decades of the twentieth century, no one outside of the fields of jazz and blues was taking such freedom with tone production and distortion. The idea that you could capture the roar of the tiger and frame its fearful asymmetry in commercial band music was a revelation.

A few years later, King Oliver gave record buyers a taste of what an authentic African American band from New Orleans could do. His 1923 recordings stand out as milestones in modern music history. Yet, here again, a modern listener would be puzzled at why they get so much attention. Oliver's cornet solo on "Dipper Mouth Blues" (1923) was widely admired and imitated at the time, but *almost nothing happens* during the solo—at least from the perspective of current-day jazz. If you look at the music written on the page, it seems cussedly simple-minded. Oliver plays the same phrase over and over again, with only the slightest variation. The whole solo uses just seven different notes—and most of it is built around only two of them.

Ah, but listen to *how* Oliver plays the notes. By shrewdly manipulating his trumpet mute, Oliver could take a single note, an E-flat in this instance, and work wonders with it. He could turn it into a sensual moan, an aggressive growl, a bemused wah-wah, or a baby crying for Mama. The narrowness in the note selection hardly matters—in fact, it makes Oliver's achievement all the more impressive. Music of this sort must have spurred a personal epiphany among countless fans (and certainly musicians) of that era.

Here's a revealing story. In 1946, jazz broadcaster Richard Hadlock arranged to take a saxophone lesson from New Orleans pioneer Sidney Bechet. Hadlock's account of this session is invaluable, if only because very few of the people who created early jazz ever tried to convey what they did in a codified manner. Perhaps a few of them gave music lessons, but we can only speculate on what advice they gave their students. Yet if Bechet's tutelage of Hadlock is any indicator, the New Orleans inventors of jazz had strange notions about how to teach music. "I'm going to give you one note today," Bechet told his surprised pupil. "See how many ways you can play that note—growl it, smear it, flat it, sharp it, do anything you want to it. That's how you express your feelings in this music. It's like talking."[1]

"I'm going to give you one note"? Playing it is "like talking"? Could this really be how one learns to play jazz? The mind boggles at such pedagogy. But in the extraordinary musical scheme created by Bechet and his contemporaries, a whole universe of significations could be contained in that single note, and the masters of the idiom were expected to find a seemingly infinite number of ways of expressing them. They did this better than anyone had before—at least within the confines of Western commercial music. Prevailing conceptions of pitch (playing in tune) and timbre (playing with a proper tone) were challenged and eventually toppled by the African American insurgency. The jazz art form was constructed in large part upon this subversive attitude.

What about more modern or even avant-garde jazz players? How would they fit in with Sidney Bechet's aesthetic vision? Music critic Zan Stewart shares an interesting conversation he had with the parents of Eric Dolphy, one of the leaders of the jazz avant-garde during the 1960s. They mentioned that Eric would sometimes devote an entire day to playing a single note.[2] The more things change, the more they stay the same!

So the dictum that listening to jazz begins with paying attention to the individual notes is more than just some facile truism. This is hardly a matter of identifying the names of the tones in a jazz solo and writing them down on music paper (a skill that few fans possess but, happily, isn't a prerequisite for getting deep into the music). You could stare at those for days and still not grasp the essence of jazz. Much of the essence of this idiom is conveyed by precisely those elements that can't be captured on a musical score. Rather, I'm claiming that, just as scientists first split the atom open in 1917 (the same year as the first jazz recording, by the way), the New Orleans musicians of that same period split open the notes of Western music. In both instances, energy was released, and you can be the judge of which left behind the biggest bang. The later evolution of American music existed embryonically in the freedom the first jazz artists took with tone production. In later decades, they would take many more liberties with their craft, but all these were perhaps anticipated by the bold pioneers of Bechet's day, who decided that you could do "anything you want" to the notes.

It's hardly a coincidence that this 'tune and tone' revolution was spurred by American musicians of African ancestry. The African tradition conceptualizes music-making as the creation of sounds. You may think that music-making is *obviously* the creation of sounds, but that's not really the case. The Western performance tradition of the last two millennia has been shaped by practitioners who conceptualized music as a system of *notes*—of discrete tones, tuned in scales with twelve subdivisions. Back in the days of Pythagoras, Western musicians had to choose between creating sounds and playing notes—and they opted for the latter. But African musicians never got enlightened (or is *corrupted* the better word?) by Pythagorean thinking. They followed the other path—creating a music that drew on infinite gradations of sound, and not just twelve notes in a scale. The musicians of the African diaspora eventually learned how to coexist with the Western schema, but not before they had forced some changes on it. The African sensibility clashed with the Western systems of music, and both were forced to give ground. Yet how much richer we are for this give-and-take! In later chapters we will deal with the 'bent' blues notes and the other mind-expanding ways of tone distortion African Americans contributed to our musical vocabulary. But even at this early juncture in our story we see almost every implication of this revolution in Sidney Bechet's instructions to his pupil: *Growl it, smear it, flat it, sharp it, do anything you want to it.*

The mandate of the listener is the mirror image of this admonition. Don't just listen to the notes; listen to what the great jazz artists do to them. As part of your musical education, seek out the jazz players with the gnarliest tones

and the least polished sounds. A good starting point is Duke
Ellington's band: no composer in history understood better
than Ellington the potential for mixing an African conception of tone production with Western systems of orches-
tration. Once again, this is not empty praise or a formulaic
compliment, but a very key building block of his legacy
that deserves your closest attention. You can hear this aspect
of his genius as far back as the mid-1920s, and by the dawn
of the 1940s he had completed the Herculean task of incorporating a vital and unapologetic African sensibility into
the heart of American popular orchestra music. In track after track, he showed what a happy marriage between Western note systems and non-Pythagorean sound systems can
produce—wonders that neither alone might achieve. We
can still learn from his example.

By the way, this tells you why Auto-Tuned vocals on
many contemporary records sound so shallow and lifeless.
It's almost as if everything we learned from African American music during the twentieth century was thrown out
the window by technologists in the twenty-first century.
The goal should *not* be to sing every note dead center in
the middle of the pitch—we escaped from that musical
prison a hundred years ago. Why go back? In an odd sort
of way, much of contemporary pop music resembles opera,
with all the subtle shadings of bent notes and microtonal
alterations abandoned in the quest for mathematically pure
tones. In theory, software should be able to re-create all
the nuances of analog Africanized sound, but judging by

the pop records I hear, we are still a long way from realizing that goal. Maybe we need an injection of Africanized soundscapes—let's even call it a new jazz revolution!—all over again.

One last observation before moving on: I've noticed a recent change in attitude toward tone production in the jazz world. More than ever before, jazz horn players seem to prefer hitting the notes flawlessly—perfectly in tune, right in the center of the pitch, correctly aligned with the beat, with a smooth, even delivery. This prevailing sensibility doesn't have a name, so let's just call it *the new way of phrasing*. We can speculate about the reasons for this paradigm shift. Have these musicians been influenced by the Auto-Tune ethos? Or is this quest for clarity of tone part of the academic codification of jazz techniques? Perhaps the systematization of jazz and the wide dissemination of method books and teaching manuals, filled with precise notation of examples, have played a role in this process. I have no deep-seated objections to this approach; many of my favorite jazz artists over the years have opted for a similar kind of clean, crisp, on-the-mark phrasing. But whenever any technique becomes too pervasive, the time is ripe for a new generation to shake things up. As you develop your own listening skills, try to gauge which tendency is in the ascendancy. Are musicians playing the notes with precision, almost as if they are reading music from some Platonic ideal score, or are they handling them roughly, torturing them to make them speak the truth?

Dynamics

Jazz musicians have much to teach us about 'tone and tune,' and in the paragraphs above I happily praised them for their ability to impart a universe of subtle significations to even a single note. But we now move on to the subject of *dynamics*, and here I am forced to take a more critical stance. I am perhaps a tough taskmaster on this matter. "Dynamics" refers to variations in volume of a note or phrase; in classical music, a number of Italian words have been adopted to describe these shifts, from *pianissimo* (very soft) to *fortissimo* (very loud), and you can tell quite a bit about the flavor of a concert piece by how many *p*s and *f*s you see on the written score. Jazz composers also do this, but given the improvisational nature of jazz, many decisions on dynamics are made spontaneously on the bandstand.

This can prove challenging. In the heat of performance, musicians often find it difficult to agree on a change from loud to soft, or vice versa, and unless they are listening closely to each other and are intimately in sync, the result is often long stretches without much dynamic variation. When I encounter a group that seems capable of making these shifts—whether because the musicians have carefully rehearsed them or simply because these adaptations have become an instinctive part of their musical telepathy (I especially admire the latter)—I am quick to give them credit for skill in handling one of the thorniest issues of the jazz trade.

To the outsider, dynamics must seem like the simplest aspect of music. Either you play louder or softer, or you stay the same. What can be so hard about that? Yet in the context of jazz, this is much more problematic than the outsider realizes. Jazz is a hot art form. It thrives on intensity. For better or worse, a macho aesthetic got embedded in its DNA at an early stage in its evolution. As a result, louder is almost always the easier option on the bandstand, especially for inexperienced performers. Some jazz ensembles have pursued cooler approaches over the decades, but these have tended to go against the grain of the idiom, and this tendency also brings with it risks and downsides. Add to these the difficulty in coordinating dynamic shifts in real time in an art form built on spontaneity and assertiveness, and the result can perhaps be expected. Fortissimo is the preferred declamatory stance, and pianissimo performers get blown off the bandstand. Sure, there are exceptions, especially at slow tempos, where the musicians are more willing to bring down the volume level. But at a medium-to-fast pace, jazz music is usually loud and in-your-face. Done with skill, this can work, and even work brilliantly, but when handled clumsily, this kind of unvarying aggression quickly proves wearying. Audiences burn out on unrelenting volume, whether it's a politician shouting out denunciations on the campaign stump, a preacher bellowing a lengthy fire-and-brimstone sermon, or an amateur jazz band full of testosterone and determined to conquer the world. In this regard, I like to quote a favorite aphorism from Oxford art historian Edgar Wind: "Mediocrity which claims to be intense has a peculiarly repulsive effect."[3]

Let's be fair and acknowledge that other musical idioms also have predispositions in dynamics. This isn't the place for a discussion of the volume of pop and rock music, but a historian of the music could profitably pursue that subject. Classical musicians are perhaps the most focused on subtle dynamic shadings. But, frankly, I believe that many classical performers are too extreme in this matter—the soft passages are too soft, the loud passages too loud. In their zeal to show their skill at shifting dynamics, they exaggerate the fluctuations, and the performances sometimes seem capricious, like a conversation in which your interlocutor moves from shouting to whispering, abandoning communication in favor of a series of outlandish postures.

So I don't expect (or even want) a jazz band to emulate the approach of most classical ensembles. But I do want to hear jazz musicians make an attempt to control the dynamics, rather than letting the dynamics control the music. As part of your musical education, you should listen to jazz bands that have risen to the challenge and actively use dynamics as a tool in shaping the performance. For example, check out the Ahmad Jamal trio tracks from the 1950s, and marvel at a group that could swing with fervor at very fast tempos, yet with such control over the volume that you can hear every nuance. (Start with the YouTube video of Jamal performing "Darn That Dream," filmed at CBS Studios in New York in December 1957, which still leaves me gobsmacked every time I watch it.) Or listen to how pianist Erroll Garner used surprising changes in dynamics to enliven his solos—few, if any, have done this better in the history of the art form. Or hear how Art Blakey could shape the volume of a jazz performance even while conveying the impression that the band was almost out-of-control, swinging madly in sweet intoxication from the music. Or, best of all, study the recordings of the Modern Jazz Quartet, an ensemble that may have been better at employing dynamics as a means to creative expression than any group in the history of jazz. Then take what you learn from this listening, and apply it to the next jazz band you hear, whether in concert or on record or streaming on the web. Does it measure up or fall short?

Personality

This book aims to take you inside the music, and you probably think that requires deep technical understanding of music theory. But my contention is that most of the key elements in music, even in something as apparently arcane as jazz, can be grasped without advanced training. We won't ignore the technical parameter in these pages—they inevitably come to the forefront in some subjects, for example, in any discussion of jazz harmony or compositional structure. But even when we encounter a thorny technical issue, we can turn to metaphor and analogy to convey much of its significance to a non-musician. The bottom line: most of the jazz idiom is accessible to anyone willing to approach it with patience and open ears.

In fact, the deepest aspect of jazz music has absolutely nothing to do with music theory. Zero. Zilch. This bedrock layer of improvisation, almost beyond the scope of musicology, is the psychology or personality of the individual musician. The mathematical ratios that underpin music are the same for every player, yet each one will approach a jazz solo differently. This is especially true for the most advanced musicians, for whom technical issues no longer present an obstacle—their mastery allows them to focus more on self-expression. In a very real sense, assessing performers who are operating at this high level is akin to grappling with their characters and psyches.

Long ago, I reached a conclusion about jazz musicians that some might find highly controversial and others accept as so obvious that it hardly needs to be stated. I've never heard it mentioned, although I think it provides a highly useful perspective on listening to the music, so I will share it for your consideration. During my own apprenticeship years, I noticed that if I met musicians before I heard them perform, I could frequently predict how they would improvise. Their personality in off-stage interactions got transferred into how they approached their solos. A brash, confident person would play with assertiveness and flamboyance on the bandstand. The quiet, cerebral types would reflect those same qualities in their music. The jokester would impart a dose of humor to the performance. The sensitive and melancholy players would gravitate to songs that displayed those selfsame attributes. A jazz improvisation is, in a very real sense, a character study or a Rorschach test. So much so that I could even imagine, with vivid precision, how non-musicians—friends, family members, coworkers, and the like—might improvise if *they* played jazz.

This intensely personal quality to improvisation, its tendency to mirror the psyche, may be the most enchanting aspect of jazz. What a joy to hear those moments when the music dispenses with all pretense, and reveals its psychological truths, the musician speaking from the heart, and those in the audience serving as witness! I have so much faith in this essential *translucency* in the music that I trust the songs more than biographical facts. Anecdotal evidence, for example, makes clear that Miles Davis was a difficult, often hostile individual; he could be rude, or outrageous, or perhaps even violent. But the music tells me a different story about Davis, and while I don't dismiss the tales about his bad side, I know that these accounts can't capture the whole truth. He couldn't have made that body of music if he didn't possess, *at the deepest level*, a predisposition to tenderness and vulnerability. Perhaps the rudeness was a cover for that vulnerability, a protective screen. I have no evidence for this beyond Davis's music, but I know that his music possesses its own honesty, a truth as reliable as biography or memoir.

For the same reason, I can't accept the premise of the Oscar-winning film *Amadeus* (based on Peter Shaffer's play), which tells us that Mozart was an infantile dork but also a profound genius. Novelist William T. Vollmann, in his novel *Europe Central*, does the same thing in his portrayal of the composer Dmitri Shostakovich, whose sober and draconian music is shown as originating in the Russian master's immaturity, perhaps even buffoonery. These depictions, albeit entertaining, fail to convince. They simply can't be true. I cannot reconcile the music with the character displayed on screen or in the pages of a novel. We rightly call on the music itself as persuasive, sometimes even irrefutable, evidence. It serves as a type of polygraph test, a source of insights about its creator that anecdotes or colorful after-the-fact reconstructions cannot invalidate.

Perhaps all of us seek this kind of intimate revelation when we listen to music. I dwell on it here at some length because I want to urge newcomers to jazz to use this element of expression as an inviting entry point into the music. Even before you grasp the technical complexities, you can hear this element of self-expression. When I praise the artistry of, say, a Charles Mingus or a Lester Young or a Bill Evans, it is in large part due to the fact that their music has brought me into some kind of relationship with them. I never met them, but I feel I know them—and with an unshakeable certainty that is, to some degree, a measure of their greatness as jazz artists. I'm sure many other jazz fans feel this connection with the artist and share my conviction that this is not just a listener's subjective reaction but a valid response to profound elements in the music. I should add that when I have spent time around a major jazz star, such as Dizzy Gillespie or Dave Brubeck, the experience has confirmed my view. These people proved to be precisely the kind of individual I expected to meet, based on their music-making.

By the same token, I sometimes hear artists who convey little or nothing about their personality and character through their music, and I can't help but feel that this is a warning sign. I can hypothesize many causes for this barrier between the music and the creative spirit who performs it. The most obvious reason why musicians fail to put a personal stamp on a jazz performance is technical limitation: they simply lack the effortless mastery of the idiom that is necessary for self-expression. Their solos show them wrestling with the demands of the song rather than turning it into a platform for their personal vision. But I've also encountered the opposite extreme: musicians who are so skilled at mimicking different styles and idioms that they never find their own voice. Individuals of this sort may even have great success in the music world; this kind of imitative skill is invaluable in a session player who wants to earn a living in Los Angeles, Nashville, New York, London, or some other center of recording activity. But these performers will fall short of greatness in jazz, an art form that not only allows personal expression but demands it.

At this juncture, a few readers will raise objections. It has become quite fashionable in recent decades to emphasize the essential subjectivity of our responses to works of art. Trendy critics have developed a whole vocabulary to express this point—cumbersome terminology that conveys their "anti-foundationalism," or their antagonism to "privileged" interpretations, or their insistence that works of art are mere *simulacra*, a kind of representation drained of authenticity or connection back to an originating impulse. Theoretical discussions of this sort are beyond the scope of this book. But I must say in passing, before moving on, that everything I've experienced in jazz, whether as performer, critic, or fan, rebels against this attitude. If only from a practical perspective, it represents an impoverished way of listening to music. By their own admission, critics who adopt this extreme subjectivity are merely *listening to themselves*. If you learn anything from this guide to listening, let it be a respect for the demands of the music—a realization that understanding jazz (or any other form of artistic expression) can never be reduced to personal whim or some flamboyant deconstructive manipulation of *signifiers* but always builds on a humble realization that these works impose their reality on us. The work of art always requires us to adapt to it—and in this manner can be distinguished from escapism or shallow entertainment, which instead aims to adapt to the audience, to give the public *exactly* what it wants. We can tell that we are encountering a real work of art by the degree to which it *resists* our subjectivity.

Spontaneity

This final ingredient in the jazz mix might be the most important of them all, but it's devilishly difficult to isolate and describe. More an attitude than a technique, the element of spontaneity in the music rebels against codification and museum-like canonization. Indeed, the instant you try to hold onto it—to re-create the tones and phrases that spontaneity has imparted to a jazz performance—is the very second when it disappears. Yet this frame of mind, the openness to the creative possibilities of the present moment, is perhaps the defining aspect of the jazz idiom.

All human learning and experience can be divided into two groups, and you can tell a lot about people based on which of these opposed realms they prefer to inhabit. On the one hand, we have experiences that always repeat themselves with unvarying sameness—this is the realm of science, mathematics, and deductive reasoning. When the experiment is repeated, it produces the same results. On the other hand, we have those experiences that will never be repeated. This is the realm of the poetic and miraculous, the one-time event that won't come around again. That's the universe that contains your first kiss, the moment of your child's birth, and all the other singular incidents that, even in an age of digital backup and copy-and-paste, refuse replication. Jazz belongs to that miraculous realm. When the jazz experiment is repeated, it *never* produces the same result.

A revealing story is told of bassist Charles Mingus, who led some of the most creative jazz bands from the 1950s into the 1970s. When one of his band members succeeded in playing an especially exciting solo that generated lots of applause from the audience, Mingus would yell at him: "Don't do that again!"[4] The puzzled musician might think, at first, that the bandleader was jealous of the acclaim. Was Charles Mingus angry at getting upstaged by a hired hand? Maybe so. But eventually the perceptive musician would grasp the hidden profundity in the boss's warning. When you play a crowd-pleasing solo, the temptation is to try to re-create the same phrases at the next performance, and the next one after that, and so on. But a kind of rigor mortis sets into jazz when improvisers start down that enticing path. Instead of capturing the heat of the moment, they are left trying to rekindle the embers of gigs long departed. "Don't do that again" may well be the most potent jazz mantra, a guidepost for the musician who seeks the highest peaks of artistic transcendence.

You can't measure that spontaneity in a jazz performance. But you can feel it. And you especially notice it when it's gone. Of course, some skeptics insist that this element in the music is so intangible that you can't tell with any certainty when it comes and goes. But that simply isn't so. If you see the same jazz musicians play a song on several different occasions, you eventually figure out how much spontaneity enters into the proceedings. And if you still aren't sure whether a musician is really improvising, just ask the other members of the band. I assure you that they know. But after you have developed your listening skills in jazz, you probably won't need to make such inquiries. You will feel it in the music and cherish it as the most magical part of the jazz idiom.

If you don't, you can always leave the jazz club and check out a rock or pop covers band. That's perfect entertainment for people who want to live in the realm of perfect replication. Jazz, in contrast, is for those who want to be in attendance when the miracle happens.

THREE

The Structure of Jazz

A JAZZ PERFORMANCE CAN BE CONFUSING TO THE UNINITIATED. Even many hard-core jazz fans find aspects of the music mystifying. They struggle to identify a melody or discern an underlying structure to the music. Songs sometimes change direction suddenly and unpredictably. Different musicians in the band take charge at unexpected junctures—the focal point moves from saxophone to trumpet to piano to bass or other instruments—but seemingly without rhyme or reason.

What's going on here?

We've all heard that jazz musicians improvise. But does that mean they just make it up as they go along? Is it possible that there is no real structure to this music? Is jazz just a free-for-all, like those wild moments in TV wrestling when all rules are abandoned, the referee ignored, and every combatant goes for broke? Or is there method to this apparent musical madness? Is jazz more like a chess match—but played much, much faster—in which creative freedom is bound by rules and imagination must operate within carefully defined constraints?

In truth, jazz is a little like both those examples. Sometimes it feels like hand-to-hand combat on the bandstand, but it can also get as cerebral as a room of grand masters debating the best way to achieve checkmate. Rules define almost every aspect of the music, but they are applied flexibly, and sometimes can even be ignored. Much of the beauty in the music draws on this creative tension.

Newcomers to the music immediately grasp the freedom in jazz. The sense of liberation in this music is so palpable that jazz has often been embraced or censored as a symbol of political freedom and human rights. We are all familiar with lyrics getting banned because they broached some taboo subject, but how can instrumental music serve as an ideological rallying cry? Yet the Nazi leaders feared the influence of jazz music, as did the overseers in the Soviet Union and other totalitarian regimes. During the German occupation of France in World War II, jazz guitarist Django Reinhardt needed to get approval from the Propaganda-Staffel before each performance for the songs he planned to play. And Nazi fears were not without justification: after "La Marseillaise" was banned, Reinhardt's jazz song "Nuages" was adopted as an alternative song of rebellion by the French resistance movement. Among the citizenry, jazz stood as the antithesis of repressive rules.

Yet jazz has its own rules—although not repressive ones—and they can be elusive, hard to grasp, especially from the perspective of a newcomer to the music. But a serious fan can't really appreciate what happens during a jazz performance without some understanding of these structural underpinnings and how they are applied in practice.

The vast majority of jazz performances follow a familiar pattern. You might call it "theme and variations." You can divide the song into three parts. First, the musicians play the melody (or theme). Second, they improvise over the harmonies of the song—with some or all of the performers taking solos (these are the variations). Third, the musicians return to the melody for a final restatement of the theme. Not every jazz performance follows this blueprint—and in some extreme cases, the musicians follow *no set pattern*—but more than 95 percent of the jazz music you will encounter in recordings or live concert will adhere to this theme-and-variations structure.

The themes are of set duration. Frequently, they are thirty-two bars long with four beats in each bar, especially when the piece in question is a jazz standard drawn from the classic American song repertoire of George Gershwin, Cole Porter, Irving Berlin, and other mid-twentieth-century tunesmiths. But song lengths of other durations aren't uncommon. Twelve-bar forms are especially popular, most notably in blues songs (we will learn more about them later). But when a song is fairly short, say twelve or sixteen bars in duration, the musicians typically play the melody twice at the beginning and conclusion of the performance. These three options—thirty-two-bar songs, twelve-bar songs, sixteen-bar songs—account for the vast majority of the jazz performed since the early 1930s. True, you will occasionally encounter jazz compositions that deviate from these patterns—especially in recent years, when many jazz players are trying to move beyond the popular song structures that have long dominated jazz. Also, the earliest jazz composers, back in the 1920s, favored more complex patterns for their compositions. But those exceptions can't obscure the fact that a few simple structures account for most jazz music performed since its inception.

We are getting off easy, my friends. If this were a book on the symphony, our heads would spin under the weight of the jargon and charts necessary to explain the organizational precepts and their major variations. If this were a listener's guide to fugue and counterpoint, you would have probably tossed it in the trash can ten pages ago. But jazz isn't like that. It draws on the same basic structures we find in many pop songs. If you can count to thirty-two and keep the numbers in time with the beats in the music, you are ready to roll. You can follow along with the music, and always know where the musicians are in the underlying structure.

You have Thomas Edison to thank for all of this. It's hard to envision jazz flourishing without Edison's invention of sound recording technology, which made it possible to preserve and disseminate musical improvisations for the first time in history. But this same technology also imposed severe structural constraints on jazz compositions. Musicians turned to simpler structures because recordings in the early days couldn't capture more than about three minutes of music. Before the rise of jazz, African American composers worked extensively with more complex forms. Most of Scott Joplin's ragtime pieces relied on four separate sections, each with its distinctive melody and chords, and many of the earliest jazz musicians continued in this vein. If you play a song of this sort fast enough, perhaps you can finish it in just under three minutes; but even if you win this race, will you have any time left for improvised solos? I marvel at the recordings Jelly Roll Morton made in the 1920s, in which he tries to retain the comparatively complex structures he had learned from the rag composers and still leave a little space for improvisation. But few jazz artists had the skill to pull this off; and even more to the point, most of them preferred to feature their solos on record rather than demonstrate mastery of complex compositional forms. Something had to give, and that usually turned out to be the song structure. If a band kept to twelve- or thirty-two-bar songs, they still had time for several solos before they ran out of 'disk space.' A few renegades resisted this process of simplification—most notably Duke Ellington, who continued to work with elaborate structures even when his contemporaries were embracing simple riff tunes. But he was a rare exception. Most jazz artists in those days before the long-playing (LP) album were content to draw on pop songs and blues, and even when they wrote their own material, they borrowed the uncomplicated structures of those genres.

The most common thirty-two-bar song form in American twentieth-century popular music and jazz is AABA. The two themes—A and B—are each eight bars long. The B theme, which offers a countermelody in a contrasting key, is sometimes called the "bridge" or "release." It provides a dose of aural variety before returning to the final eight-bar A theme restatement. Another familiar thirty-two-bar structure features a sixteen-bar single melody played twice, but with a slight variation between the first ending and second ending. And simplest of all, as mentioned above, are the many jazz songs that rely on a single theme, usually of twelve or sixteen bars, repeated without variation. These are child's play compared with the typical form for a Scott Joplin ragtime piece from the early 1900s, which presents four different sections in the sequence AABBACCDD. Or check out Duke Ellington's structure for "Sepia Panorama" from 1940, which briefly served as his band's theme song (later replaced by "Take the 'A' Train"). It relies on four themes arranged in the unconventional sequence ABCDDCBA.

Here is what Ellington serves up on this three-minute-and-twenty-second track:

SEPIA PANORAMA

A theme (12 bars) Dialogue between orchestra and bass
B theme (16 bars) Dialogue between reeds and brass
C theme (8 bars) Dialogue between orchestra and bari-
tone sax
D theme (12 bars) Blues improvisation featuring piano
and bass
D theme (12 bars) Blues improvisation featuring tenor
sax
C theme (8 bars) Dialogue between orchestra and bari-
tone sax
B theme (8 bars) Dialogue between reeds and brass
A theme (12 bars) Dialogue between orchestra and bass
Coda (2 bars) Concluding passage played by bass

This work reminds me of a palindrome, a word or phrase spelled the same forward and backward. *A man, a plan, a canal—Panama!* Or *Won't I panic in a pit now!* In other words, the opening theme in Ellington's piece is also the final theme, the second theme is also the second to last, and so forth. The only deviation from perfect symmetry here is the abbreviated restatement of the B theme—which is only eight bars long. I suspect that Ellington would have preferred to stay with the sixteen-bar version he had used earlier in the track, but he probably feared that he would have run beyond the time constraints of a 78 rpm record.

Yet you wouldn't guess any of this from a casual hearing of the song. It only becomes obvious when you analyze the structure.

Ellington, of course, could write successful hits in standard AABA form, but these always coexisted with his ambitious plans for more elaborate compositions—not just more complex songs, but also suites, musical dramas, and tone poems. None of his peers and few of his successors could match Ellington's skill at tinkering with the formal structures of jazz. Of course, some influential critics belittled these ambitions. "The whole attempt to fuse jazz as a form of art music should be discouraged," complained composer Paul Bowles after the Carnegie Hall debut of Ellington's most visionary work, the three-movement suite *Black, Brown & Beige*. Even a few devoted fans grumbled that Ellington was abandoning jazz and should return to the accepted formulas for commercial swing band hits. Ellington was clearly discouraged by responses of this sort, and he never attempted another work on the same scale as *Black, Brown & Beige*. But history has validated his vision. Jazz is accepted as art music everywhere, even at Juilliard and Carnegie Hall, and young jazz musicians in the twenty-first century are increasingly adopting complex formal structures that bear more than a passing resemblance to those Ellington devised more than seventy years ago.[1]

The detailed outline of "Sepia Panorama" shared above is typical of the material I present when I teach jazz to college students. Before I play the music, I describe the structural milestones in the piece they are about to hear. Then we go through the work in question—ideally several times—and see how the structure is realized in actual performance. For many students, this is a revelation. True, they already knew that musical works are built according to rules, but they usually assumed that these rules can't be understood without years of musical training. They aren't entirely wrong. Some aspects of jazz do require that kind of in-depth study. But most of the key elements of musical structure in a jazz performance can be grasped even without resorting to musical notation. In fact, some of the most crucial aspects of a performance—for example, tenor saxophonist Ben Webster's robust and breathy tone control in his "Sepia Panorama" solo—could never be notated using our conventional Western systems for writing down music. So I don't rely much on musical scores when teaching jazz appreciation. As in the outline above, I stick with simple ABCs. And this is an alphabet well worth learning. You can hardly grasp the importance of an artist such as Duke Ellington without probing his bold ingenuity in manipulating these discrete sections into profound musical utterances.

Let me offer two more 'music maps' to guide you through the structure of some well-known jazz tracks. First, let's look at "Sidewalk Blues," recorded by pianist Jelly Roll Morton and his Red Hot Peppers in Chicago on September 21, 1926.

SIDEWALK BLUES

Preamble   Spoken repartee with whistle and car horn sound effects

Intro   (10 bars) Comprised of 2-bar introductions for each of the main instruments: piano (2 bars), trombone (2 bars), cornet (2 bars), clarinet (2 bars), and finally the entire band (2 bars)

A theme   (12 bars) Blues-based melody played by cornet and the band supporting with stop-time accompaniment on beats 2 and 4 of each bar

B theme   (12 bars) Different blues-based melody with different chords played by the ensemble

A theme   (12 bars) Improvisation played by clarinet with band providing stop-time accompaniment on beats 2 and 4 of each bar

Interlude   (4 bars) Transitional passage played by the ensemble leading to

C theme   (32 bars) Melody played by the ensemble, interrupted at bar 15 by the car horn

C theme   (32 bars) Melody played by three clarinets until the final eight bars, when the rest of the band enters playing improvised New Orleans counterpoint

Coda   (6 bars) Concluding passage played by the ensemble followed by unaccompanied car horn

You could enjoy this track even without analyzing the structure, but you will have a much better grasp of Morton's artistry and aesthetic vision if you take the trouble to explore the formal properties of his music. A casual listener would probably consider this a novelty song, perhaps even an undistinguished one, especially given the corny dialogue and sound effects. In fact, Morton is often dealt with, even in some jazz books, as a shallow showman, noteworthy for his flamboyant demeanor and fashion accessories—his diamond tooth, his stylish wardrobe, his braggadocio, his underworld connections—rather than for his compositional skills. The whistle and car horn in this track seem to substantiate this focus on flash over substance. But don't be misled by the gimmicks. Jelly Roll Morton is also one of the most brilliant formalists in the history of jazz, as "Sidewalk Blues" demonstrates.

In this instance, we see Morton's peculiar decision to mix twelve-bar blues forms with thirty-two-bar song forms. This is an unusual choice: I suspect that 99 percent of the jazz performances that feature a twelve-bar blues chorus keep on repeating it for the duration of the song. Moving from a blues structure to a sixteen- or thirty-two-bar structure in the middle of a performance creates a dramatic moment of disjunction in the proceedings, but in Morton's capable hands it sounds perfectly natural and aesthetically satisfying. You may remember that we just saw a similar mixture of blues and song structures in Ellington's "Sepia Panorama." Indeed, there are many similarities between these two artists' approach to jazz, but you would miss almost every one of them if you didn't probe into the underlying construction of their music. In "Sidewalk Blues," Morton fortifies these melodies with two separate introductions, one with speech and sound effects—nowadays we might call this *musique concrète*, but that term wouldn't enter the vocabulary of performers for another two decades—and a second one featuring all of the key solo instruments. Morton is equally ingenious in coordinating the accompaniment, relying on breaks (short two-bar solo statements with the band playing on the first beat of the first bar) and stop-time (a complete solo with the band supporting only on certain beats, in this instance on beats 2 and 4 of each bar).

But most surprising of all, to my mind, is the three-clarinet section toward the conclusion of "Sidewalk Blues." Jazz bands of this period usually relied on a single clarinet player, and even Morton followed this formula for most of the recording session. Yet he hired two additional clarinet players for the date, even though they only had a few seconds of music to perform. To a seasoned fan of early jazz, this shift in texture is much more shocking than any of the novelty effects on the track. In the 1930s, jazz groups would start featuring reed sections of this sort, but here Morton is anticipating the emergence of the big band back in the mid-1920s.

Finally, I would call attention to how little space Morton allocates to improvisations by his band members.

Improvisation usually accounts for the vast majority of a jazz performance, but Jelly Roll pursued a different vision for his combo music. He sought a more holistic sound in which the individualism of each performer was occasionally on display but mostly subservient to the collective wisdom of the ensemble and (especially) the compositional vision of Morton himself.

An anecdote about this artist adds some useful background to what we see in the structural unfolding of his recordings—and also illustrates why he was often remembered for his edgy behavior. During a 1920s recording session, Morton got into a heated argument with trombonist Zue Robertson over how to play one of the pieces. Robertson had his own way of interpreting the song and stubbornly insisted on it even when his boss, who was both composer and bandleader, got in his face. How was the disagreement resolved? Morton reached into his pocket and pulled out a large pistol, which he placed on top of the piano. On the next take, the trombonist played the melody exactly as Morton had written it. Some commentators see this as a colorful story about Jelly Roll's criminal leanings, but I prefer to view it as a sign of his commitment to an austere and demanding musical vision.

Next, let's move two decades forward and explore "Night in Tunisia," recorded by alto saxophonist Charlie Parker in Hollywood on March 28, 1946. Compared to the Ellington and Morton tracks, the form here is much simpler: most of the performance follows the familiar AABA format. But we encounter a few deviations from the form, most notably an intricate twelve-bar interlude before the solos, an ingenious progression composed by Dizzy Gilles-pie (who is not featured on the track) that leads into a virtuosic four-bar solo break by Parker. Try counting the sixteen beats in those four bars, and you will appreciate the subtlety with which the altoist seems to break free from the underlying beat, even as he never loses sight of it. This brief solo break stands out as the emotional centerpiece of the performance, but you will enjoy it all the more by grasping the structural elements that contain it. In essence, the break serves as a disruptive juncture between the com-posed and improvised sections of the track, and much of its potency comes from the contrast with the stately interlude that precedes it. (By the way, you also get to hear a very young Miles Davis playing trumpet on this track.)

NIGHT IN TUNISIA

Intro   (12 bars) First 4 guitar, next 4 bass and drums enter, final 4 horns enter

A theme   (8 bars) Melody statement played by muted trumpet (Miles Davis)

A theme   (8 bars) Melody statement played by muted trumpet

B theme   (8 bars) Melody statement played by alto sax (Charlie Parker)

A theme	(8 bars)	Melody statement played by muted trumpet
C theme	12 bars)	Interlude played by the ensemble
Solo break	(4 bars)	Unaccompanied break played by alto sax
A theme	(8 bars)	Improvisation by alto sax
A theme	(8 bars)	Improvisation by alto sax
B theme	(8 bars)	Improvisation by trumpet
A theme	(8 bars)	Improvisation by trumpet
A theme	(8 bars)	Improvisation by tenor sax
A theme	(8 bars)	Improvisation by tenor sax
B theme	(8 bars)	Improvisation by guitar
A theme	(8 bars)	Melody played by alto sax
Coda		Same as intro, fade after 4 bars

By following music maps of this sort, newcomers to jazz begin to grasp that a style of music that initially sounds unconstrained and almost formless—the performers seemingly operating in the absence of rules, like gunslingers in a Wild West town without a sheriff—actually builds on a finely tuned balance between freedom and structure. Every jazz composer and band approaches this trade-off differently. A few, such as Jelly Roll Morton and Duke Ellington, willingly sacrifice a great deal of individual freedom in exchange for the creative potential inherent in structure. Others, such as John Coltrane in his final years, take the opposite approach, seeking musical transcendence by breaking away from structures, in some instances refusing to accept any limitations on where the spirit of the moment might take them. In practice, most jazz artists operate between the extremes of formalism and spontaneity, searching for the right kind of blueprint for a performance, an underlying architecture that guides and inspires without feeling burdensome.

After studying a few jazz tracks in this way, listeners will be able to construct their own music maps. In the meantime, there are a few places beginners can go for guidance. I strongly recommend *Jazz: The Smithsonian Anthology*, a collection of classic recordings that includes detailed descriptions of song structure for more than one hundred tracks and other useful background information. (Full disclosure: I contributed some of these track guides.) Those who can read music should also check out the growing number of online videos that provide note-for-note transcriptions of solos—or in some instances, of entire tracks—on-screen in tandem with the recording. I wish these resources had been available when I started studying jazz. I can recall so many instances in which I asked myself: What's really going on in this music? I remember the long hours spent trying to unlock many of the mysteries (as they seemed to me at the time) inherent in this art form. Now everything is laid bare with just the click of a mouse or the touch of a screen. Don't hesitate to take advantage of these resources.

Each of the recordings considered so far is played in 4/4 meter—in other words, it proceeds in units of four beats, and listeners who want to follow the structure can count along in time with the musicians. This meter has dominated the jazz world since the 1930s, and shows no sign of falling out of favor. As you expand your listening horizons, and open your ears to the full range of jazz available in performance and on recording, you will inevitably encounter music in other meters. Almost every jazz band nowadays performs some jazz waltzes—in 3/4 time (or, in other words, with three beats per bar)—in its repertoire. The jazz waltz was a rarity until the late 1950s, but now it's a staple of the art form. When Dave Brubeck popularized 5/4 meter with his immensely successful recording of Paul Desmond's composition "Take Five," the use of this time signature was considered by some as a novelty, a one-time experiment that few others would imitate. But nowadays 5/4 has entered into the mainstream of the music. Odd meters are perhaps not quite commonplace in twenty-first-century jazz, but they are hardly gimmicks. In fact, you can find jazz songs in almost any conceivable meter nowadays, and increasingly I encounter bands that change meters at multiple junctures during a single song or, in extreme cases, in every bar.

Sometimes the musicians graciously give listeners a hint in the title of the song. Paul Desmond's "Eleven Four" is, as you might guess, in 11/4 meter. Pat Metheny's composition "5-5-7" relies on two bars of five beats followed by a bar of seven beats. Denny Zeitlin's song "At Sixes and Sevens" moves back and forth between six-beat and seven-beat bars. In most instances, however, musicians don't serve up clues of this sort. Yet with careful listening, you can learn to identify the meter of even unconventional forms. The Internet is your friend in this endeavor—the web is awash with commentary and background information on specific jazz tracks, and without much effort you can find examples of various atypical meters and use them as counting exercises.

In a pinch, if you are trying to figure out what is happening musically in an especially complicated work, you can always reach out to the musicians. Jazz performers tend to be obliging when approached by someone who wants to get a better grasp of their work. They aren't pop celebrities like Kanye West or Justin Bieber, with an entourage of bodyguards and handlers keeping the public at a safe distance. You can reach out to them, and they almost always respond. I don't hesitate to email musicians and request explanations or even copies of charts. And others approach me about music I've recorded. I recently contacted a jazz composer for help in identifying the structure of a recorded track, and he sent back a written score that showed not only frequent metric changes during the course of the song, but also that the various musicians in the band weren't always playing the same meter at the same time. The drummer's time signature was different from the bassist's, and so forth. Until I saw the score, I couldn't hear what was really happening with the performance. Even the pros can find it daunting to 'reverse engineer' a work of this sort, so newcomers to jazz shouldn't be too disturbed when encountering songs in which the metric structure is hard to pin down. But rest assured that the vast majority of jazz, even in the new millennium, stays true to the old four-beats-to-the-bar formula—and newbies can quickly learn to feel those 4/4 bar lines without having to count them.

Before moving on, let me offer a few more suggestions about how to improve your ability to hear the metric structure of jazz. First, when trying to get the 'feel' of the pulse you may find it easier if you follow the bass player. Most people assume that the drummer sets the beat for the band, and so they try to lock into the underlying beat by focusing their attention on the percussion. Perhaps seventy or eighty years ago, this would have been a smart listening strategy. But the drums in jazz have evolved away from timekeeping—in truth, much of the action in jazz percussion these days happens *between* the beats—and thus can serve as a confusing guide to those seeking something akin to a metronome for their listening sessions. Bassists in jazz are hardly immune to this evolution away from timekeeping, but they tend to be more straightforward in signaling the pulse in a song. In many instances, they will play on every beat, bar after bar—the so-called walking bass line—and this provides both a pleasing forward motion to the performance as well as a useful guide to those counting along in the audience.

But your listening experience will be even more enhanced if you listen to the pulse in larger units—trying to
feel the two-bar and four-bar units of the work as rhythmic building blocks for the performance. Since the rise of
Kansas City jazz in the 1930s (discussed later in this book),
most jazz has tended to move ahead, or perhaps I could say
metaphorically that it *breathes in and out*, in four-bar increments. You may have noticed that the most common structures for jazz—twelve-bar, sixteen-bar, and thirty-two-bar
forms—are each divisible by four. Jazz musicians (and audiences) recognize, even if only unconsciously, the aesthetic
pleasure that comes from the symmetrical foundations of
the idiom, even as the musicians' improvisational creativity
imposes new rhythmic superstructures on this base.

Jazz players aren't prime number folks. Even today, when
a soloist exchanges phrases with the drummer, the give-
and-take almost always proceeds in four-bar increments.
Jazz musicians actually describe this as "trading fours." And
when they occasionally deviate from this norm, it is typically to trade eight bars or twelve bars or sixteen bars—not
groups of three or five or seven. The same is true when
two horn players get into a sax battle. The exchanges will
usually evolve into a dialogue of four- or eight-bar phrases.
The sax phrases don't always start neatly on the first beat of
bar 1 and end on the last beat of bar 4, but even when they
deviate markedly, the sense of this underlying structure can
still usually be felt in the music. For this reason, listeners

can benefit from trying to conceptualize many jazz performances as an unfolding of four-bar units. At a certain point in your listening you will stop thinking about the individual beats and bars, and begin to feel these larger building blocks. You know you have reached this point when you instinctively sense when the four bars have concluded without having to count the individual beats.

A good way of hearing jazz in this manner is to listen to tracks in which soloists exchange four-bar phrases with the drummer or with each other. Check out, for example, the recording "Tenor Madness," a well-known sax battle between Sonny Rollins and John Coltrane recorded on May 24, 1956. Here, in the context of a straightforward twelve-bar blues form, the horns take extended solos and eventually engage in four-bar exchanges with each other, as well as with drummer Philly Joe Jones. Or study "The Chase," another horn battle between saxophonist Dexter Gordon and Wardell Gray, recorded live in concert on February 2, 1952. Here the two combatants exchange full thirty-two-bar choruses and then trade off on sixteen-bar half choruses, moving on eventually to eight- and four-bar give-and-take. Or check out "Blues Walk" recorded by the Clifford Brown / Max Roach Quintet on February 24, 1955, which features my all-time favorite trumpet versus tenor sax battle—here Brown and tenorist Harold Land even get down to exchanging bars and half bars. Or enjoy the various recorded tenor sax battles between Zoot

Sims and Al Cohn, longtime colleagues who spent many years engaged in symmetrical jousting of this sort. Listening closely to these tracks, and others like them, will train your ears to hear jazz as more than a sequence of isolated phrases and to grasp the underlying structures that support the artists' creativity.

FOUR

The Origins of Jazz

W HERE DID ALL THIS COME FROM? YOU MIGHT THINK THAT THIS would be a fairly easy question to answer. Jazz is a modern urban music that first came to the public's attention in New Orleans during the early years of the twentieth century. Even in my own lifetime, many people who participated in the birth and evolution of early jazz were still alive—and they were quite willing to share what they knew about these events. In other words, there should be few mysteries about circumstances so recent and so influential.

Yet the origins of jazz are as perplexing as the unsolved enigmas surrounding Homer, Shakespeare, and other long-distant innovators in the history of culture. Even with such a recent story, we are forced to rely on rumor and conjecture. Buddy Bolden, often acknowledged as the first musician to play jazz, left behind no recordings, and even the basic facts of his life and career have been hotly debated.

Jazz probably flourished for two decades, more or less, before the first African American bands were recorded in the early 1920s, but our understanding of this period is sketchy at best. Even the word *jazz* has a puzzling etymology—it first appeared in print in a newspaper article about baseball!—and it's still a controversial term among practitioners of the art form.

We can't afford to ignore this embryonic stage of the music's development, despite the obscurity of these origins. Even today, jazz is shaped by the priorities and perspectives—and, indeed, the paradoxes—of its earliest practitioners. They were both entertainers and artists, and didn't seem to worry much about the potential for conflict between these roles. They were representatives of a folkloric tradition but also exponents of a sophisticated new city music that prided itself on its audacity and innovations. They mastered a wide range of preexisting styles—including blues, rags, marches, and dance music—while trusting in their ability to make up something new on the spot that would depart from established models. We can still hear all of these conflicting agendas play out in jazz music today.

But the first generations of jazz musicians also participated in a bold project of social experimentation and innovation that went far beyond the bandstand. Even back in the 1920s, they were realigning attitudes toward race and culture, proving to anyone paying attention that jazz could spur integration and cooperation—all this long before other spheres of American life dealt with their own issues of prejudice and bias. We perhaps shouldn't be surprised when a crowd-pleasing performance style influences social life, but jazz seemed to have a special destiny in this regard. It celebrated human agency and personal autonomy to a rare degree, but also channeled the creative expression of an ostracized underclass. The combination of these two seemingly incompatible factors—the heroic quality of the music and the systematic ill treatment of the people who made it—imparted particular resonance to the egalitarian elements in jazz, turning it into a powerful engine for social change. An understanding of these wider ramifications of the jazz experience is an essential part of grasping the essence and ethos of this music—even its twenty-first-century manifestations.

You can still hear the imprint of jazz's predecessors in the music today. From the blues, jazz musicians learned how to bend notes, how to play dirty, how to break away from the tyranny of the pure and ideal written notes that have dominated so much of Western music since the time of Pythagoras. From ragtime, jazz borrowed syncopation, that exhilarating sense of displacement and momentum created by putting rhythmic emphasis between the beats. In military bands and brass bands, jazz players gained proficiency with a range of instruments and eventually learned how to play old horns in new ways, literally reinventing performance techniques to suit their own whims and needs. At social gatherings and dances in turn-of-the-century New Orleans, these pioneers of jazz learned how to take these various ingredients and make them serve as the building blocks for a new form of popular entertainment suitable for crossover success. Jazz performers are still aiming to do all these things today.

Then as now, jazz musicians were scavengers and borrowers, visionaries who broke through the boundaries between highbrow and lowbrow, religious and secular, caste and clan. Historians of the music give the most attention to the influence of blues and ragtime on the evolution of early jazz, but a host of other styles and sounds played a role in the creation of this exciting new hybrid. The earliest jazz performers also took note of the sounds of the sanctified church, the stately music of concert halls and opera houses, the popular dance tunes played by string ensembles—indeed, anything that came to their attention and might excite an audience.

And here's the beautiful part of the story: jazz musicians still beg, borrow, and steal, only now they do it on a global basis. Today we hear exciting jazz in the current moment that joins in intimate embrace with tango or salsa or the Carnatic music traditions of southern India. Or movie music, cartoon songs, the aleatory techniques of John Cage, hip-hop, electronica, country and western, folk ballads, and almost any other aural tradition you can name or conceive. All the original elements still flourish in the music—listeners still delight in the bent blues notes, those syncopated raggy phrases, the honking saxes and muted brass instruments, and that big bass drum that started out as a military tool but has evolved into the primal pulse of revelry and dance. Even in an age in which most music has gone virtual, abandoning the world at hand and descending into the realm of bits and bytes, jazz still rejoices in handmade (and mouth-made) sound. When you think about it, we really aren't all that far from the music's roots back in New Orleans. We've just added more ingredients to the gumbo.

I don't think it's mere coincidence that jazz first emerged in New Orleans. I've devoted a considerable amount of time, over the years, to studying the conditions that spur cultural innovation and the dissemination of new artistic movements, and the emergence of jazz serves as the perfect case study in how these revolutions take place.

Statisticians have developed a host of analytical tools to predict the spread of innovations, whether artistic movements or technologies or consumer products. You might be surprised to learn that these mathematical models were originally developed to predict the spread of diseases. Strange to say, new art forms are similar to the plague or a virulent flu in how they spread. Art and disease proliferate via contagion, and similar conditions favor both. Densely packed populations, many individuals coming and going via land and waterways, an overheated mixture of people recently arrived from different locales, informal settings where they intermingle in close contact, a culture and environment that emphasize communal activities and get-togethers— these are nightmare conditions for anyone trying to stop an epidemic, but they are the same ingredients that can spur world-changing artistic revolutions.

Such has always been the case. The Renaissance emerged around the same time that the Black Death spread through Florence. This devastating plague eradicated much of the city's population in 1348, and history books often date the first stirrings of the Renaissance in this city to 1350. Coincidence? I don't think so. When I researched the impact of the troubadour song in the history of Western love music, I found that this innovation moved through Europe following roughly the same pathways as the Black Death.[1] And many other artistic breakthroughs show this same correlation. For example, the age of Shakespeare was also a time of recurring plagues in England: in 1563, a year before the Bard's birth, a quarter of London's population was killed in an outbreak, and an equally virulent plague spread through the city in 1603, the same year *Hamlet* was published. We talk nowadays of cultural memes going *viral*, but this isn't just a poetic way of speaking.

Jazz followed the same formula. New Orleans, at the time when jazz first appeared, was one of the unhealthiest cities in the world. Buddy Bolden, lauded as the originator of the jazz idiom, was born in New Orleans right before the devastating 1878 yellow fever epidemic raged through the city. Black infant mortality in New Orleans at the time was 45 percent, and the typical life span of an African American a mere thirty-six years. The first jazz records were released shortly before the 1918 flu epidemic decimated the city. Dance halls were closed and streets emptied as people sought refuge in their homes or in other healthier locales. Louis Armstrong, later recalling that "everyone was down [with the flu] except me," took a job playing country dances fifty miles outside the city, in Houma, Louisiana.[2] Pops Foster, the pioneering New Orleans bassist, remembered playing gigs while wearing mosquito nets over his head. All cities had to deal with public health risks, but New Orleans was especially dangerous, no doubt because of its particular mix of well-traveled residents, climate, population density, and poor local sanitation.

These selfsame conditions gave birth to jazz. No urban area on the planet offered a more diverse cultural mix during the years leading up to the emergence of jazz than New Orleans. Here was the perfect setting for viral musical memes, circa 1900. A visitor to the city at that time could hardly help noticing its French and Spanish heritage, its African and Caribbean connections, and its constant interactions with the rest of the United States resulting from its prominent location at the gateway of the Mississippi. Every thing was mixed together; everything was in flux. New Orleans was the melting pot within the larger melting pot of American life. And when vibrant cultural traditions are forced into such close interaction and exposed to so many disparate influences, exciting new hybrids invariably emerge from the mix. In this instance the result was jazz, a distinctive performance style created by black Americans who drew on—and added to—the extraordinary musical

ecosystem of turn-of-the-century New Orleans. When we
listen to the ways new millennium jazz mixes effortlessly
with Latin and Caribbean currents, or with the formal
structures of Western classical music, we are experiencing a
continuation of the cultural dialogue that presided over the
idiom's birth.

Of the many ingredients that contributed to the birth
of jazz, the most important was the blues. This is especially
surprising when one considers that blues music was virtually unknown to the American public at this time. The
recording industry didn't discover the blues until 1920,
when Mamie Smith's recording of "Crazy Blues" became
a surprise hit and introduced many listeners to a style of
song that had remained almost completely hidden from
public view in previous decades. Only a few professional
musicians in the Deep South, and even fewer outside observers, had paid attention to this raw and rule-breaking
idiom during the early days of the twentieth century. The
blues were mentioned in a handful of turn-of-the-century
documents—almost always in hints and allusions with few
specifics—and by 1912 its distinctive harmonic progression
had found its way into a few pieces of published sheet music. Yet jazz musicians in New Orleans not only had heard
and grasped the significance of the blues by this point, but
had already made it a centerpiece of their own hybrid work.

We are so familiar with blues music today that we take
its innovations for granted. Long ago the blues spread beyond the world of African American performance idioms

and came to play an important role in rock, country, soul, and a host of other styles—in fact, when my son started playing viola in a string orchestra at age twelve, one of the first pieces his ensemble performed was a twelve-bar blues. In this regard, his experience was not much different from that of countless guitarists, keyboardists, and other instrumentalists: the blues is now a starting point in the education of aspiring performers. This perhaps conveys the misleading impression that it is a simple genre, suitable for beginners, and hardly a world-shaking music innovation.

But the world of song was much different in the year 1900, and almost everything about the blues represented a radical break with the past. The twelve-bar blues song structure itself was a striking deviation from the norm, but even more remarkable were the *bent notes*, those tones that wavered and swooped and refused to accept the constraints of conventional musical notation. For almost 2,500 years, Western music had prided itself on staying in tune, on working within the structures of carefully defined scales and intervals, the *do-re-mi-fa-so* building blocks that underpinned every song. But African music had never bought into this paradigm: it operated within a universe of *sounds*, not discrete *notes*. These two approaches might seem irreconcilable, but black Americans found a way of making them coexist, first in songs of worship and labor and recreation, and eventually in the sphere of commercial music—especially in the blues. In a blues song, the performer both plays the note and refuses to play it, and this new freedom of intonation stirred listeners, especially with its bold movement between consonance and dissonance, even between major and minor tonalities—previously distinct soundscapes that now coexisted in the same phrase, the same notes that refused to be mere notes.

How did New Orleans performers discover this sound long before anyone in the music publishing business and nascent recording industry knew about it? The blues at this juncture rarely appeared in large cities; the most likely place to hear it in the early 1900s would be agricultural regions of the South where black sharecroppers and rural workers resided. I own a copy of an old almanac from the 1920s, and a map in it highlighting the regions of African American farming is almost identical to a scatter plot of the birthplaces of the earliest known blues musicians. But around this time, Jelly Roll Morton recalled hearing a woman named Mamie Desdunes, who lived next door to his godmother in the Garden District of New Orleans, singing this blues song:

> If you can't give me a dollar, give me a lousy dime.
> Can't give a dollar, give me a lousy dime.
> I wanna feed that hungry man of mine.[3]

Here we encounter the typical lyric structure of the blues, which in its early evolution was primarily a song for voice with minimal accompaniment, perhaps a single instrument played by the vocalist—only in later years would instrumental blues without words become commonplace. A blues chorus was built on three lines, each four bars long. (Perhaps I should say *approximately* four bars long: early blues performers would occasionally add or subtract a few beats, as the mood hit them. But you won't hear that very often nowadays, when even blues players deeply immersed in the tradition keep strict track of the bar lines.) The opening line was repeated, and then followed by a rhyming line. Each of these three lines was typically delivered in tandem with an instrumental response, a few blues notes that fill up the final beats of each four-bar unit.

In its earliest days, this accompaniment was most often provided by guitar, but the pioneering blues musicians developed brazen new ways of playing this instrument. In order to create the distinctive bent notes of the blues, they scraped the strings with an oddball assortment of makeshift items—the blade of a knife, a glass bottleneck removed from the bottle and wrapped around a finger, a filed-down steak bone. Here again, the goal was to subvert the Western scales, to break free from the isolated, self-sufficient notes of fretted instruments and explore the sounds that existed beyond the borders of these defined tones.

The first jazz performers grasped, with remarkable insight, that this music could be played on brass and reed instruments, and in this fashion serve as the key ingredient in a boisterous new style of dance music. In some instances they continued to feature blues as vocal music, but they also understood that it had extraordinary power as a purely

instrumental idiom, with a horn filling the central role previously held by the singer. Even more striking, they grasped
that these bent blues notes could also be incorporated into
non-blues songs; in fact that almost any tune could be enlivened by applying the distinctive intonation of the blues
to a melody, whether written or improvised. At the dawn
of the twentieth century, this way of conceptualizing music
represented a tremendous advance, a cultural breakthrough
as important as anything happening in the concert halls of
Paris, London, or New York.

But one more building block was required to give jazz
its mojo, and this was *syncopation*. "Syncopation" refers to
a deliberate disruption in the flow of the music, typically
achieved by placing rhythmic emphasis between the beats.
The simplest syncopations can be taught to children—they
quickly learn how to clap along with "The Charleston" beat,
which spurred a dance craze in the 1920s with its repeated
accent midway between beats 2 and 3 of the bar. Even basic
syncopations of this sort possess a hypnotic appeal, imparting
both propulsion and disjunction to the flow of the music.
Children find it satisfying to clap along with this syncopated
rhythm, and so do grown-ups. This sound draws listeners to
the bandstand and dancers to the floor, and even in a digital
age, when many music fans are jaded and think they've heard
it all before, a song that smartly incorporates syncopation can
use it as a hook to climb the charts.

Unlike the blues, syncopation was no secret to American music fans at the turn of the century. The technique

can be traced back to the Middle Ages, and over the centuries many composers had employed it in various ways to enliven a work. But in the early twentieth century, ragtime composers were employing syncopation with a degree of intensity and rhythmic virtuosity that music fans had never encountered before. They liked what they heard, and turned ragtime into a huge commercial fad.

Scott Joplin stands out as the greatest of these ragtime composers. His most influential work, "Maple Leaf Rag," was a sensation after its release in 1899, and provides a striking example of the power of syncopation. Joplin can't really be considered a jazz artist, but he is still important for our purposes as one of the key forerunners of the music. I learned how to play many of his pieces as a youngster, and mastering ragtime rhythms helped me enormously when I later turned my attention to jazz. (A side note: When I later entered Stanford as a freshman, I played "Maple Leaf Rag" as my piano audition piece—although the judge was expecting something by Beethoven or Chopin; it is a testimony to how much attitudes have changed that such a decision, at the time, still had the power to shock music professors. I passed the audition but left the room feeling that I had violated some unspoken rule.) Perhaps if Joplin had lived longer, he would have developed ties to jazz players. But, in a historic irony, he died a few days after the release of the first jazz record in 1917. In his lifetime, he tried to advance beyond the formulas of ragtime, but in his mind this meant drawing on elements of classical music in shaping new ways of presenting a distinctive African American approach to composition. As far as we can tell, he had little interest in (or awareness of) the techniques employed in New Orleans to blend rag phrasing with bluesy intonation and improvisation.

But if Joplin didn't know about jazz, jazz musicians knew about Joplin and the other ragtime composers. Jelly Roll Morton, in a recording he made toward the end of his life for the Library of Congress, demonstrated how he 'jazzed up' Joplin's music—his before-and-after comparison is a revelation. The syncopations are still prominent, but the approach is more spontaneous and carefree, the rhythmic momentum looser, the beat more danceable. Here, in a brief four minutes of music, we can hear how the seeds of ragtime sprouted into the unfettered creativity of New Orleans jazz.

Joplin and Morton both were pianists, and the ragtime revolution took place primarily on the keyboard. But even before the rise of jazz, brass bands and other ensembles took rag music and adapted it for other instruments. New Orleans musicians embraced this idiom with fervor and also saw the potential for applying its essential elements to new purposes. They started using the term "ragging" to refer to any instance in which lots of syncopation was inserted into a song, and it didn't need to be a ragtime piece; any kind of music, from a funeral dirge to an opera aria, could be ragged.

Who was the first musician to put these ingredients together to create jazz? According to the most knowledgeable observers, this innovator was Buddy Bolden, an African American horn player born in New Orleans in 1877. Bolden played the cornet, similar to the trumpet but more compact and usually marked by a mellower tone—although no one would ever use the word "mellow" to describe Bolden's sound. He made a name for his strident music in the Crescent City at the turn of the century, and one of the few things almost every source agrees on is the loudness of his playing. But there are huge gaps in our knowledge about this individual and his music, as well as the process by which he developed his approach to jazz. No recordings of his band have survived, and despite rumors to the contrary, none may have been made. Some secondhand accounts of Bolden's life and times were collected by early jazz writers, but these are often contradictory, and a few have been disproven by subsequent research. As far as we can tell, newspaper writers only paid attention to Bolden when he got in trouble with the law—as happened in 1906, when he was arrested for assault, an incident probably related to his incipient mental illness. The following year he was committed to the Louisiana State Insane Asylum at Jackson, where he remained until his death in 1931 at age fifty-four. He never gave an interview or spoke with any jazz researcher, and probably died unaware that he would enjoy posthumous acclaim as one of the great musical innovators of the twentieth century.

Can we believe the legend? We live in a skeptical age, and fanciful stories of a single person inventing jazz, whether in a moment of brilliant insight or even gradually over a period of time, invite serious doubt. And the careful scholar can identify a large number of people who contributed, in various ways, to the emergence of this exciting new performance style. Even so, I am convinced that Bolden did something momentous in turn-of-the-century New Orleans. The old-timers may disagree over the facts of Bolden's biography, but the awe and fascination this musician inspired among both the public and fellow performers suggests that he was forging something new and different, transgressive and intoxicating. Put simply, I have no disagreement with those who laud him as the father of jazz.

Like other jazz fans, I would love to have a recording to substantiate this, but the descriptions from those who heard Bolden leave little doubt about the key ingredients of his playing. "Buddy Bolden is the first man who played blues for dancing," insisted bassist Papa John Joseph, born in 1874. "He played a lot of blues," confirmed Peter Bocage, another New Orleans cornetist born in 1887. "Blues were their standby. Slow blues." "He played all kinds of numbers, including many blues," later commented Wooden Joe Nicholas, a New Orleans cornetist born in 1883 who modeled his own style on Bolden's. He added, "He played everything, every piece that came out." Tom Albert, another New Orleans cornetist born the same year as Bolden, described the latter's group as "about the best, a ragtime band, with the blues and everything." Clarinetist Alphonse Picou, born in 1878, made special mention of Bolden's ability to rag tunes, noting that "he was best at ragtime." But the surviving accounts also make note of Bolden's singing. In fact, his most famous number, "Funky Butt," was an irreverent vocal piece. Celebrated New Orleans clarinetist Sidney Bechet, who claimed that Bolden's group was "the best in New Orleans," explained that "the police put you in jail if they heard you singing that song."[4]

These scattered descriptions give us a good starting point for the next stage in our listening guide, where we look at the evolving styles of jazz. Yet even here, in the very first stirrings of the music, we find in microcosm the essential building blocks of the jazz idiom. Bolden and the others who participated in this revolutionary movement drew on the full range of music available to them, but especially the blues. They married this blues sensibility to the rhythmic vitality of ragtime, and adapted both these idioms to the horns and other instruments available to them in turn-of-the-century New Orleans. And all of this was infused with an irreverence and willingness to break the rules that ensured that this new style wouldn't stand still, but continue to morph and change and advance. Even today, more than a century later, we can hear all of these elements in jazz music. All of us involved in the jazz enterprise are still, unmistakably, the progeny of Buddy Bolden and his Crescent City cohorts.

FIVE

The Evolution of Jazz Styles

FEW PEOPLE KNEW ABOUT THIS EXCITING NEW STYLE OF MUSIC UNTIL the release of the first jazz recordings in 1917. The Original Dixieland Jazz Band enjoyed a huge hit with its recording of "Livery Stable Blues," which reportedly sold a million copies—an extraordinary success when one considers that a Victrola cost a month's wages at the time, and only a half million of these record players were purchased that same year. Almost overnight, jazz went from a little-known regional performance style to a coast-to-coast craze.

Jazz fans are often reluctant to celebrate this milestone event. The ODJB was a white band that built its popularity on an idiom created by blacks, and its famous hit record, with its fanciful imitation of animals on the horns, must have struck many listeners as a corny novelty rather than the advent of a pathbreaking art form. Yet the impact of this debut jazz recording can hardly be doubted.

It set up a tumult that quickly reconfigured the shape of American commercial music, paving the way for a host of other bands to make their own records and build an audience—so much so that the next decade is remembered as the Jazz Age.

The term "jazz" itself still stirs up controversy among musicians. Many embrace it with pride, but others find it demeaning and seek out alternative ways of describing this musical revolution. These debates are complicated by the fact that it is hard to determine with any precision what the term meant to the people who first applied this label to the music. The word "jazz" first appeared in print in a 1912 California newspaper, where it referred to a wobbly baseball pitch that batters had trouble hitting. Over the next few years, the term spread into the popular discourse, and came to attach itself to almost anything new and vibrant in the culture. A journalist in 1913 tried to define jazz, and I find his litany of related meanings both maddeningly convoluted and perfectly suited for describing the essence of the musical phenomenon it now designated. "A new word, like a new muscle, only comes into being when it has long been needed," explained Ernest J. Hopkins in an article entitled "In Praise of 'Jazz,' a Futurist Word Which Has Just Joined the Language." He went on: "This remarkable and satisfactory-sounding word, however, means something like life, vigor, energy, effervescence of spirit, joy, pep, magnetism, verve, virility, ebulliency, courage, happiness—oh, what's the use?—JAZZ."[1]

We still hear this "spirit, joy, pep" in jazz music today, but the music has changed enormously since the dawn of the Jazz Age. In fact, the music's evolution has proceeded at such a dizzying pace that jazz fans often maintain allegiance to a particular decade or style—mystifying outsiders, who wonder whether jazz music from 1950 can really be so different from jazz from, say, 1940 or 1930. But in the heated world of twentieth-century improvisation, even five years can encapsulate a world of difference. In 1959, the modal sounds of Miles Davis's *Kind of Blue* album captured a fresh, different vibe and pushed the art form forward into a new direction. This project showed how jazz improvisation could be based on tightly defined scales (or modes) and thus achieve effects not possible via the expansive chord-based improvisations of earlier jazz ensembles. But put away *Kind of Blue,* and listen to Albert Ayler's *Spiritual Unity* from 1964 in its place, and you now feel as if you are dealing with a revolution of an entirely different kind. Davis was constructing a new attitude toward scales, but only a half decade later Ayler was jettisoning modes and embracing unmediated sound in which even the very notion of a 'note' was questioned and found wanting. Yet, by the same token, compare *Kind of Blue* with albums made five years earlier—classic tracks by Clifford Brown, Max Roach, Art Blakey, or even Miles Davis's own work from 1954—and you can't help marveling over the great leap forward it represented at the time. Such tectonic shifts were typical of the jazz world during the middle decades of the twentieth century. Every revolution generated a counter-revolution; every breakthrough left audiences asking, "What's next?"

Given this state of affairs, I am hardly surprised that one of the first questions jazz fans ask upon meeting is, "What *kind* of jazz do you listen to?" At various junctures in the music's history, the jazz audience has even splintered into hostile camps—the so-called jazz wars—in which proponents of one style denounce and ridicule advocates of another. In retrospect, these tensions often seem overblown and pointless. After all, why can't a fan like both New Orleans jazz *and* bebop, or East Coast bands *and* West Coast bands, or fusion *and* avant-garde? Does enjoyment of one style require callous dismissal of another? Yet in the heat of the moment, fans (and no doubt the musicians themselves) often feel that any successes enjoyed by the other camp must come at their own expense, almost as if music were akin to a sports league in which only one team gets the championship and everyone else is consigned to the ranks of losers. Yet jazz is hardly like that, and chances are you will enhance your pleasure as a music lover by casting your net as widely as possible, and opening your ears to fresh sounds and approaches.

Fortunately this infighting has lessened in the current day. The last two decades in jazz have seen a spirit of diversity and pluralism on the rise, a tolerance of different approaches unprecedented in the music's history. Even so, a guidebook of this sort can hardly ignore the often radically diverging approaches to jazz that have flourished at various points during the last century. Yes, I may love *both* New Orleans jazz and bebop, but I definitely listen for different things in these two idioms. With this in mind, I offer here a compact guide to the major styles of jazz, explaining their defining characteristics and sharing what qualities I look for in these different approaches to the music.

New Orleans Jazz

It all begins here. And even though so much has changed in jazz since its early days, the art form still bears the stamp of the New Orleans pioneers. Let's take one example: Back in the 1920s, Louis Armstrong literally invented new musical phrases and an approach to improvisation that still can be heard today all over the world. In fact, his influence is hardly limited to the jazz world but can be detected in the work of countless performers in other idioms. Most of them are probably unaware of Armstrong's role in their own artistic lineage, yet they are indebted to the musical vocabulary he introduced long before they were born. If his heirs could collect royalties on all these borrowed licks, the Armstrong estate would rank among the wealthiest of them all.

But we need to start our examination of New Orleans style before Armstrong made these changes. In its earliest manifestation, this music was a collective effort. Indeed, classic New Orleans jazz is perhaps the most team-oriented sound in the genre's history. Heroic individualism, akin to that later advocated by Armstrong, had a much smaller role in this music back in those distant days before 1925. The most characteristic moment in these earliest jazz performances comes when all of the horns join together in spontaneous counterpoint, a give-and-take that requires each player both to stand out as an individual and blend into a larger whole.

This typically involves three horns. The cornet (or the trumpet) plays declarative melodic phrases, rich in syncopation, in the middle register. The trombone supports with forceful outbursts in the lower register. The clarinet adds ornamental phrases and jazzy comments in the high register. This often happens at the same time, and though you might think the proceedings will collapse into an ugly cacophony—how can three horns, played with such abandon, not get in each other's way?—somehow the ingredients not only cohere but, when played by skilled musicians, positively sparkle.

This is, in my opinion, the most joyous sound invented during the entire course of twentieth-century music. Jazz has certainly changed since these early innovators came on the scene, and perhaps, as some assert, it has gotten better. Certainly jazz has become more complex. But I would never dare assert that jazz has ever reached a higher rung of gaiety and excitement than we encounter here, in its first manifestation back in New Orleans. The phrase that comes to mind is "irrational exuberance"—a term once used by Federal Reserve Board chairman Alan Greenspan (a former jazz saxophonist, by the way) to describe an overheated stock market, but that, to my way of thinking, ought to belong to the city of New Orleans as a motto for its music.[*]

Yet virtually from the start, a creative tension can be felt in jazz. At almost every juncture you can hear musicians trying to find a balance between asserting their individualism, developing their distinctive solo voice, and working within the constraints of a collective sound. In the middle years of the 1920s, Louis Armstrong tilted the balance. Compare the 1923 recordings of King Oliver's Creole Band, where Armstrong is still mostly held in check and blends in with the rest of the band, with his brash trumpet pyrotechnics on "West End Blues" from 1928. In just five years, jazz evolved from a balanced team sport to a platform for extroverted individual soloists. It never looked back. Even today, when bands play New Orleans–style jazz, they leave plenty of room for individual solos.

When listening to this music, I find it fascinating to gauge the different ways musicians address this creative tension. Jelly Roll Morton, whose work we studied back in Chapter 3, was a strict formalist, or at least as close to that as we will find in the loose-and-easy world of jazz. He allowed his musicians to take solos, but only in small doses, with the distinctive personalities of the band members subservient to the holistic quality of the performance. At the

---

[*]Greenspan played clarinet, sax, and flute in his youth, and considered a career as a jazz musician. But in his midteens he played in an amateur band alongside Stan Getz, who was a year younger than the future Fed chief. After comparing his skill level with his soon-to-be-famous bandmate's, Greenspan decided that economics was a more suitable calling.

other extreme we encounter the many followers of Louis Armstrong, who emulated his individualistic approach and helped establish it as the norm for jazz.

The explosion of Armstrong's genius during the late 1920s is so dazzling that a listener might be tempted to focus just on his pathbreaking tracks from this period. They certainly demand the attention of any serious student of jazz, and we will have occasion to discuss them again later in this book. But you can't really understand Armstrong's breakthrough if you don't pay close attention to earlier recordings, nor will you grasp the essence of the jazz revolution as it swept through American music in the years following World War I. My preferred starting point for a chronological survey of jazz history is with King Oliver's recordings of "Dipper Mouth Blues" and "Froggie Moore," both recorded in 1923. Oliver takes a celebrated cornet solo on the former, but allows his protégé Armstrong to solo on the latter. In both these instances, the improvisation still blends in with the sound of the other instruments. Jazz at this time is still mostly a group effort.

But now compare these with Louis Armstrong's solo on "Potato Head Blues" from 1927 or "West End Blues" from 1928. Remember my claim above that jazz revolutions took place every five years, more or less? Well, here is a perfect example. By the late 1920s, we have arrived at the heroic age of the jazz soloist, and at this moment in time Louis Armstrong is ahead of everyone else in the inventiveness of his improvisations and the ease with which he executes his musical ideas. The basic building blocks of New Orleans sound remain, and we still occasionally encounter the irrational exuberance of three-horn counterpoint, but most of the performance is now devoted to individual solos. More to the point, Armstrong carries everyone with him into this brave new world. Not just the bandleader but even the supporting players are increasingly judged on the basis of their prowess in stepping forward as featured soloists.

By the end of the 1920s, this changeover was complete. During this same period, jazz had expanded far beyond its breeding ground in New Orleans. Hot music gained traction as a national phenomenon, a soundtrack for an era that F. Scott Fitzgerald would dub the Jazz Age. In particular, the music now flourished in Chicago, New York, and the other major American cities. In each new setting, jazz found a host of local adherents and continued to morph and evolve as both an art form and a commercial enterprise. But even though jazz refused to remain static—indeed, was destined to evolve beyond the stylistic tendencies of the New Orleans pioneers—many fans still prefer these sounds from the music's earliest days.

NEW ORLEANS JAZZ:
RECOMMENDED LISTENING

Louis Armstrong, "Heebie Jeebies," February 26, 1926
Louis Armstrong, "Potato Head Blues," May 10, 1927

Louis Armstrong, "Struttin' with Some Barbecue,"
    December 9, 1927
Louis Armstrong, "West End Blues," June 28, 1928
Sidney Bechet, "I've Found a New Baby," September 15,
    1932
Sidney Bechet, "Wild Cat Blues," June 30, 1923
Johnny Dodds, "Perdido Street Blues," July 13, 1926
Freddie Keppard, "Stock Yards Strut," September, 1926
Jelly Roll Morton, "Black Bottom Stomp," September 15,
    1926
Jelly Roll Morton, "Sidewalk Blues," September 21, 1926
King Oliver, "Dipper Mouth Blues," April 6, 1923
King Oliver, "Froggie Moore," April 6, 1923
Original Dixieland Jazz Band, "Livery Stable Blues,"
    February 26, 1917

Chicago Jazz

Chicago jazz draws heavily on the New Orleans tradition.
That's hardly surprising when you consider that many of
the leading New Orleans jazz musicians moved during
the 1920s to Chicago, where their techniques and songs
were closely studied and imitated by a host of Midwestern
performers. But even as they drew on these role models,
the acolytes worked to incorporate their own trademark
sounds and expand the scope of the music.

The textures of the music gradually changed in this new setting. The saxophone shows up with increasing frequency in Chicago jazz bands, sometimes as a replacement for the trombone, and imparts greater cohesion to the instrumental textures. But even when a trombone is included in the ensemble, it now acts more as a melody instrument and less as a rhythmic anchor to the proceedings. The clarinet also changes its role in Chicago, moving away from the ornamental figures of the New Orleans tradition and instead pursuing more free-flowing syncopated motifs. In many instances, the clarinetists emerge as star bandleaders or admired soloists—enjoying a prominence rarely found in early New Orleans jazz. Over the course of the decade, the banjo is replaced by the guitar; the tuba disappears from most jazz bands, and its functional role is taken over by the string bass.

The resulting sound is more streamlined, but a flashy, restless quality also enters the music, most evident in the underlying pulse. The drums in New Orleans style keep a steady pulse, but the Chicago bands deliberately disrupt the rhythmic flow, for example, adding cymbal crashes and heavy bass drum hits on the last beat before the start of a new section of the song—a technique known as "the explosion." The "flare-up" can also occur at the end of a section: here the horns hold a chord, and the drummer pauses momentarily before charging back into the fray. Bands often shift into shuffle rhythms for a brief section, to add variety to their sound, or the drummer will start accenting the backbeat heavily right before the end of a chorus. Percussion still *supports* the band's horns, but increasingly gives them a kick in the pants too—a shift in attitude that still resonates in the jazz world today.

Even more striking, the two-beat feel of the early New Orleans sound gradually morphs into a more modern four-beat pulse. Compare the King Oliver recordings from 1923 with the Red McKenzie and Eddie Condon Chicagoans' sides from 1927, and feel this subtle yet decisive shift in the flow of jazz music. This streamlined 4/4 sensibility becomes even more pronounced over the next decade, especially when the more relaxed swing of Kansas City jazz (discussed below) rises to prominence in the 1930s. Chicago jazz resides at the midpoint between these two sensibilities: it still retains hints of the *oom-pah, oom-pah* strut that jazz inherited from marching bands and ragtime, but this back-and-forth swaying rhythm is far less pronounced than we heard in the early New Orleans bands. The musicians clearly have new notions about the essence of swing, and as a result the music unabashedly moves ahead in discrete four-beat measures.

Chicago jazz musicians of this period played many of the same songs that the New Orleans performers favored, but they also diverged from these predecessors in important ways. You can still hear twelve-bar blues among the Chicagoans, but not as often as with the New Orleans bands. Instead, commercial songs by professional songwriters start entering the jazz repertoire—perhaps not surprising, when you consider that the leading tunesmiths of the day were embracing jazz with enthusiasm and composing pieces perfectly suited for the new idiom. In general, jazz and popular music were merging, and this forced musicians to find ways of infusing a syncopated, swinging sensibility into a wide range of material, including novelty tunes, society dance numbers, and romantic songs.

The biggest breakthrough came with the birth of the slow jazz ballad. Except for the occasional slow blues, jazz had been a finger-snapping, foot-stomping music up until this point. Most tempos were medium fast, more a trot than a sprint—we don't encounter ridiculously fast songs in jazz until the 1940s—but still spirited enough to get the audiences energized and shaking their bodies to the music. The idea that jazz could also be romantic and languorous was a revelation, and this innovation came not from New Orleans but the Midwest.

The first stirrings of this new, understated attitude can be heard in recordings by Bix Beiderbecke, a baby-faced cornetist—even in late career, he resembled a cherub in a Raphael painting—born in Davenport, Iowa, in 1903. Beiderbecke embarked on his jazz career in Chicago while still a high school student at Lake Forest Academy, and he soon developed a devoted following among fans and fellow improvisers. A self-taught musician with a plaintive tone on the horn, Beiderbecke introduced a more lyrical sensibility into the jazz idiom. Louis Armstrong, later recalling a

Beiderbecke performance, remarked, "I'm tellin' you, those pretty notes went right through me."[2] On recordings such as "I'm Coming Virginia" and "Singin' the Blues," Beiderbecke joined forces with saxophonist Frankie Trumbauer to create a more relaxed approach to jazz improvisation—a new way of mixing hot and cool that would influence a host of later artists.

Many of the key Chicago musicians were the children or grandchildren of European immigrants, and they added their own distinctive ethnic ingredients to the jazz mix. We hear hints of klezmer in minor key jazz songs performed by Benny Goodman and other Jewish improvisers. Violinist Joe Venuti and guitarist Eddie Lang (born Salvatore Massaro) drew on the Italian string tradition in crafting their own personal take on jazz. Singer Bing Crosby launched his superstar career while performing with Bix Beiderbecke in the Paul Whiteman band, and his own understated vocal work showed clear signs of his Irish American heritage. These artists each drew on the existing jazz vocabulary but added to it as well.

Before moving on, I should note that the term "Chicago jazz" can be misleading. Although each of these artists had some connection with the Windy City, many of them hailed from other parts of the country, and some had their greatest successes in New York or California or elsewhere. Yet Chicago deserves credit as the epicenter of this movement, the key locale where jazz pioneers inspired a diverse spectrum of younger musicians and turned hot music into a mainstream American phenomenon. Something this exciting could hardly be confined to any city's limits, no matter how expansive. But the fact that this sound spread so quickly to other parts of the nation (and soon the world) was due in large part to the synergistic forces unleashed in Chicago in the 1920s.

CHICAGO JAZZ RECOMMENDED LISTENING

Bix Beiderbecke and Frank Trumbauer, "I'm Coming Virginia," May 13, 1927

Bix Beiderbecke and Frank Trumbauer, "Singin' the Blues," February 4, 1927

Bing Crosby and Bix Beiderbecke, "Mississippi Mud," January 20, 1928

Chicago Rhythm Kings, "I've Found a New Baby," April 4, 1928

Eddie Condon and Frank Teschemacher, "Indiana," July 28, 1928

Eddie Lang and Joe Venuti, "Stringin' the Blues," November 8, 1926

McKenzie and Condon Chicagoans, "Nobody's Sweetheart," December 16, 1927

Pee Wee Russell and Jack Teagarden, "Basin Street Blues," June 11, 1929

Harlem Stride

New York has long been a magnet for new things, from the sordid to the sublime, and the exciting jazz sounds popularized in New Orleans and Chicago quickly found a receptive audience in this new setting. But Manhattan also contributed its own innovations, especially in Harlem, which served as the springboard for so many key developments in African American music during the first half of the twentieth century.

Harlem stride piano—sometimes simply called "stride" —still stands out as the most self-contained and individualistic performance style in the history of jazz. Every other revolution in the jazz idiom has taken place in the context of ensembles, where members of the band need to work together, engaging in a creative give-and-take, in order to advance to the next new thing. Even Armstrong, the greatest of the jazz heroes, always performed in the context of an ensemble. But the Harlem stride sound was something different, namely a bravura piano style that required no support beyond the ten supple fingers of its exponents.

The origins of stride style can be traced back to the ragtime piano fad that swept through the United States at the turn of the century. The stride players adopted a similarly extroverted and energetic approach to the instrument. The left hand almost always plays on the beat in Harlem stride, but is constantly in motion with its back-and-forth 'striding' between the low and middle registers of the keyboard.

On beats 1 and 3 of each bar, the left hand goes low and typically pounds out an octave or tenth before jumping up to the mid-register to play a related chord. The right hand, as in ragtime, supplies the syncopation between the beats and delivers the melodies, ornamentations, and improvisations that, in a typical jazz band of the day, would normally be the specialty of the horns. The result is an invigorating sound, combining the provocative formulas of rag with all the new techniques of 1920s and 1930s jazz—along with a few twists and turns borrowed from classical and novelty pianists of the era.

You can add other instruments to the mix if you want, but you hardly need them: played in this manner, the piano can serve as the life of the party, a self-contained musical universe that supplies an insistent ground rhythm and plenty of musical fireworks. In fact, stride piano has enlivened many a festive gathering, including the "rent parties" of Harlem during the Great Depression, where neighbors paid for admission to the revelry and the proceeds kept the landlord at bay for another month. You can hear how these settings shaped the music, which is fun and flashy, filled with virtuosic effects, but always keeping a strong beat for the dancers.

The main performers of this idiom could be just as flamboyant as the music, and when commentators speak of Harlem stride *style,* they might just as well be describing the natty attire and extroverted demeanor of its leading lights. Fats Waller, the most famous of these, ranks among the most skilled entertainers of the first half of the twentieth century, but his boisterous singing and patter never make you miss his keyboard skills. He could mix impressionistic elements drawn from classical music into his playing, or score a hit with a finely crafted pop song, but the stride aesthetic is always at the heart of his music—especially in solo piano works such as "Viper's Drag" and "Alligator Crawl."

Stride piano was an intensely competitive field, and Waller, for all his fame and record sales, faced plenty of rivals. Willie "The Lion" Smith would stand up to any challenge—Duke Ellington called him "a gladiator at heart." Any contender who wanted to challenge the Lion "had to prove it right there and then by sitting down to the piano and displaying his artistic wares." Smith would hover over the rival, puffing on his cigar and shouting out insults if he detected any signs of weakness or hesitation from the newcomer, a repartee that often concluded with a dismissive "Get up. I will show you how it is supposed to go."[3] But a host of equally gifted pianists such as James P. Johnson, Donald Lambert, Luckey Roberts, and up-and-comers like Ellington himself could also put heat on anyone challenging their authority at the keyboard. They came to call this movement the Harlem school, and many a pupil was taught and unforgettable lessons were learned. Yet the give-and-take, whether friendly or contentious, spurred all participants to bring their best game, and they collectively left behind a milestone body of work that ranks among America's lasting contributions to the evolution of keyboard music.

Pianist Art Tatum is the culminating figure in this lineage but also the most problematic. He was a great virtuoso, unsurpassed in his technical mastery and conception of jazz piano, and his approach to the keyboard was solidly founded on the bedrock of stride piano. Yet on top of this foundation, Tatum built baroque superstructures that drew from the full range of late-nineteenth-century and early-twentieth-century music. Alongside the oom-pah stride piano sound, Tatum might insert anything from boisterous boogie-woogie to rhapsodic Lisztian flourishes. Even in the new millennium, improvising pianists have hardly assimilated the full range of techniques brought into the jazz vocabulary by this extraordinary artist. But don't turn to Tatum expecting to hear stride piano in its purest form—Willie the Lion or Luckey Roberts will give you a better sense of the essence of the Harlem school. Yet Tatum still demands your attention; better than anyone, he shows how this exuberant two-fisted sound could serve as a gateway to a larger vision of American pianism, as compelling in its way as anything found in the concert halls or music conservatories of the era.

HARLEM STRIDE: RECOMMENDED LISTENING

Duke Ellington, "Black Beauty," October 1, 1928
James P. Johnson, "Carolina Shout," October 18, 1921
Luckey Roberts, "Ripples of the Nile," May 21, 1946
Willie "The Lion" Smith, "Sneakaway," January 10, 1939

Art Tatum, "I Know That You Know," April 2, 1949
Art Tatum, "Sweet Georgia Brown," September 16, 1941
Art Tatum, "Tea for Two," March 21, 1933
Fats Waller, "Alligator Crawl," November 16, 1934
Fats Waller, "Dinah," June 6, 1935
Fats Waller, "Viper's Drag," November 16, 1934

Kansas City Jazz

Even as the rambunctious sounds of early jazz were
spreading through America, a different approach to the
music was emerging in the heartland of the nation, with
the new movement's epicenter in Kansas City. Much like
their predecessors, 1930s KC jazz bands still drew dancers
to the floor with their compelling swing, but the rhythmic flow was now more nuanced and less frenetic. The
solos were more flowing, still syncopated but with greater
focus on melodic development and a willingness to risk
understatement. This was still hot music but now infused
with a pleasing sense of ease, almost carefree in its manifestations. The term *laid-back* didn't exist during the Great
Depression, but if it did, it could have described this new
jazz movement.

Each instrument in the band had to change to create
this new sound. Listen to drummer Jo Jones, long-stand-
ing member of the Count Basie band, and marvel at how
the drum kit has evolved from the predictable time-keeping

patterns of the earliest jazz bands. The beat now moves from the snare and bass drum to the hi-hat, and the effect is magical. (Soon it will become even more attenuated, as 1940s drummers discover that they can drive the band with the ride cymbal.) The pulse is insistent but more diffused and less declamatory. Jones sometimes even puts aside his sticks and plays with brushes, creating a gentle rhythmic momentum unknown to the jazz idiom's earliest practitioners.

As if to compensate for this shift, the upright bass becomes more assertive in the Kansas City bands. Check out the big sound of bassist Walter Page, and hear how he can propel the band with his four-beats-to-the-bar walking lines. This rhythmic cushion of bass and drums frees up the jazz pianists, who no longer need to play so many notes. No one grasped this new potential for the keyboard with more insight than Basie, who now uses the piano to tinkle and interject, and offers crisp rhythmic asides or sometimes even falls silent—his efforts more in response to the beat rather than stoking the fire.

The role of the horns evolved in tandem with these changes in the rhythm section. You could even say they are liberated by the confident sense of propulsion underpinning their solos. They can swing hard if they want to or choose instead to float over the beat. If they prefer to play soft, the accompaniment will adapt to this, and the same is true if they want to lift the energy level, growling and bellowing to the patrons on the dance floor.

The traditional elements of jazz are still present but artfully modified in this new setting. The blues remains a prominent ingredient in Kansas City jazz, but it is much less raw than during the days of Buddy Bolden and King Oliver. The bluesiness is streamlined and inviting, perhaps less transgressive than its earliest manifestations, but all the more suitable for a mass audience. The shift from a two-beat to a four-beat pulse, already noticeable among the Chicago jazz players, reaches its culmination with the Kansas City bands of the 1930s. You can also hear how the music tends to move ahead in four-bar units, as phrases stretch out and the pulse opens up. The beat is still insistent and the music unabashedly *danceable*, but with a more effortless quality. This evocation of casual intensity is a key part of the music's appeal.

Bandleader Bennie Moten might have emerged as the leader of this movement: the tracks he recorded for the Victor label in December 1932 serve as classic examples of the new sounds brewing in Kansas City. But Moten died in April 1935 as the result of a botched tonsillectomy, and many of his musicians migrated to a new band formed by his pianist, Count Basie. The following year, Basie brought his ensemble to Chicago and New York, and soon began recording with the Decca label. By this time, the Kansas City jazz sound was no longer a regional style but starting to influence the music of bands from coast to coast. In many ways it laid the groundwork for the rise of the

Swing Era and the tremendous popularity of jazz big bands during the late 1930s and 1940s.

But if Basie garnered the fame, his tenor saxophonist Lester Young deserves equal credit for this reconceptualization of jazz during the 1930s. Almost everything about Young's playing was unconventional. His sax tone was smoother than his contemporaries', his phrasing less driven by syncopation and more built on a melodic sensibility. All these quirks, at first derided by his peers, eventually entered the mainstream of American jazz. In some ways, Young serves as a connecting figure in the history of jazz—the link between the jazzy romanticism of Beiderbecke and Trumbauer and the blossoming of cool jazz in the 1950s. But that lineage is not entirely fair to Young, who should be praised for what he did and not just what he inspired in the future. And even though he could play with a fragile beauty (especially when collaborating with singer Billie Holiday), his music also had a trim muscularity that made him a formidable combatant in the jam sessions of the era.

Perhaps the best way of viewing Kansas City jazz is in terms of its expansion of the jazz vocabulary and the emotional range of the music. It could be intimate or rollicking, bouncy or bluesy, romantic or edgy, but with no rough edges, and always conveying a sense of sociability and fun. It's hardly surprising that, in its wake, the sound of swinging big band jazz dominated the commercial music scene and was embraced by the entire nation in the years leading up to World War II.

KANSAS CITY JAZZ: RECOMMENDED LISTENING

Count Basie, "Jumpin' at the Woodside," August 22, 1938

Count Basie and Lester Young, "Oh, Lady Be Good," October 9, 1936

Count Basie, "One O'Clock Jump," July 7, 1937

Billie Holiday (with Lester Young), "I Can't Get Started," September 15, 1938

Kansas City Seven (with Lester Young), "Lester Leaps In," September 5, 1939

Kansas City Six (with Lester Young), "I Want a Little Girl," September 27, 1938

Andy Kirk (with Mary Lou Williams), "Walkin' and Swingin'," March 2, 1936

Jay McShann, "Confessin' the Blues," April 30, 1941

Bennie Moten, "Moten Swing," December 13, 1932

Mary Lou Williams, "Clean Pickin'," March 11, 1936

Big Bands and the Swing Era

During the course of the 1920s, a number of forward-looking jazz bandleaders experimented with various techniques for performing jazz with larger ensembles. Instead of featuring isolated trumpet, trombone, and saxophone lines, bandleaders showcased entire sections of these instruments—each capable of serving multiple roles during the course of a performance or even a single song. The individual sections might play melodies or riffs (simple repeated phrases) or blend together in chords. They could support the soloist or engage in give-and-take with other sections of the band. Individual members of these expanded groups still had the opportunity to improvise—this kind of spontaneous creativity would always remain a calling card of the jazz artist—but professional bandmates at this stage were also expected to read charts and work together in playing original scores and arrangements of familiar works.

You could describe this process as the formation of a true jazz orchestra—the counterpart to what a symphony orchestra represents in the world of classical music. A cadre of visionary composer-arrangers played a decisive role in this process. Some, such as Duke Ellington, became celebrities and stars of the music of the world; others, such as Fletcher Henderson, Don Redman, and Benny Carter, enjoyed a taste of fame as bandleaders but also earned a living as freelance composer-arrangers in various settings. Still others, including Billy Strayhorn, Bill Challis, and Sy Oliver, worked almost entirely behind the scenes. But their impact can't be measured by their name recognition and is best gauged by listening to the recordings of the era, which trace the evolution of jazz from a free-flowing spontaneous music that can hardly be captured by notation into a codified, sophisticated orchestral music played by super-sized ensembles that fill up an entire stage or bandstand.

Benny Goodman did not invent this approach: the efforts of Duke Ellington, Count Basie, and Fletcher Henderson, among others, helped lay the groundwork for his subsequent success. But Goodman served as the key catalyst in introducing mainstream America to the wonders of hot big band jazz. His appearance at the Palomar Ballroom in Los Angeles on August 21, 1935, is often credited as the birth of the Swing Era. Certainly the fans' enthusiastic reaction that night—a surprising change from the tepid response to the band on earlier stops in its cross-country road trip—marked a turning point in the bandleader's career and alerted entertainment industry leaders to the commercial potential of this style of hot and insistent dance music. Soon swing jazz was heard everywhere: on radios and record players, in motion pictures, and live at thousands of ballrooms and nightclubs from coast to coast.

In guiding your listening to this body of music, I could stress its artistry and historical importance, as many have done before. But I would urge you to remember that this was also the trendiest and most popular commercial music of its day. The marvel is not so much that artists like Duke Ellington and Benny Goodman created rich and complex musical masterpieces, but that they somehow managed to do this while still selling millions of records and dominating what, nowadays, would be called pop culture. As you open your ears to the music of 1930s and 1940s big bands, pay attention to the ways these artists manage this remarkable balancing act.

Artie Shaw, who was the highest profile musician in America during the months leading up to World War II, exemplifies the tensions inherent in the new paradigm. Shaw would enjoy huge hits with some of the most intricate songs in the history of American popular music: labyrinthine pieces such as "Star Dust," with its twisting and leaping melody, or the 108-measure form of "Begin the Beguine." But he also pleased the dancers with simple riff tunes or Latin exotica such as "Frenesí," an obscure song Shaw encountered during a Mexico sojourn and turned into one of the biggest hits of the Swing Era. The public supported all of it and made possible a rare interlude in which it didn't seem quite so strange that Shaw performed with a string quartet, or Benny Goodman commissioned works from Béla Bartók and Aaron Copland, or Duke Ellington presented an ambitious jazz suite, *Black, Brown & Beige*, at Carnegie Hall. For stunning confirmation, check out the online video of Count Basie performing on Randall's Island in 1938, and marvel at a crowd of Woodstock proportions mesmerized by a serious jazz orchestra.

At no point in the history of American music has the dividing line between populist commercial music and highbrow concert hall fare been so fluid, or marked by such surprising interactions between the two. Can you imagine a modern-day pop sensation performing a Mozart clarinet concerto as a side project, as Benny Goodman managed with consummate ease? Or a chart-topping band of our own time performing a complex work by Stravinsky at Carnegie Hall, as Woody Herman's Herd did with the *Ebony Concerto*? Don't hold your breath waiting for Justin Bieber or Taylor Swift to try something of this sort.

What a remarkable moment in American popular music history. Of course, it couldn't last. Even before the end of World War II, this golden age was coming to an end. During the 1940s, slick, riff-based dance numbers and romantic ballads came to dominate the big band sound. Glenn Miller, Tommy Dorsey, and other bandleaders who specialized in this style sought a meeting point between swinging jazz and catchy pop music. And it's no coincidence that the leading popular singer of the next decade, Frank Sinatra, rose to fame as part of the Dorsey band. Miller, for his part, could have easily made the transition to the new demands of the early 1950s, when music fans sought out simpler and sweeter fare, had his life not ended in a plane crash over the English Channel in 1944. Most jazz bandleaders, however, weren't so adaptable, and few swing big bands managed to enjoy the peace and prosperity of the 1950s. By then, most had broken up or retrenched. From this point on, jazz and pop music continued to diverge and, with only rare exceptions, left behind an almost unbridgeable chasm between the two. Yet the Swing Era proved that, at least for a brief period, the two sensibilities could coincide.

Even during the height of the big band craze, small combos continued to flourish in the jazz world. If the leading orchestras thrived by pleasing dancers, the smaller jazz groups often performed in nightclubs where listeners could sit and drink rather than jitterbug to the beat. These jazz combos also put more emphasis on improvisation— they served as an ideal setting for soloists to show off their stuff—and often did without the pretty singers who were a staple of the ballroom bands. Such music might seem ill-suited for commercial success, but in an age in which jazz was the soundtrack to American life, forward-looking small bands could still enjoy surprise hits and develop a large following. Coleman Hawkins's 1939 recording of "Body and Soul" was much studied by jazz musicians but was also a runaway jukebox hit. Benny Goodman often inserted interludes of sophisticated small combo music into his performances, and his trio with drummer Gene Krupa and African American pianist Teddy Wilson not only delighted Swing Era audiences but also helped to break down racial barriers in the entertainment industry.

BIG BANDS AND THE SWING ERA: RECOMMENDED LISTENING

Tommy Dorsey, "Opus One," November 14, 1944
Duke Ellington, "Cotton Tail," May 4, 1940
Duke Ellington, "Harlem Air Shaft," July 22, 1940
Duke Ellington, "Take the 'A' Train," February 15, 1941
Benny Goodman, "Sing, Sing, Sing," January 16, 1938
Benny Goodman Trio, "After You've Gone," July 13, 1935

Coleman Hawkins, "Body and Soul," October 11, 1939

Fletcher Henderson, "New King Porter Stomp," December 9, 1932

Glenn Miller, "In the Mood," August 1, 1939

Artie Shaw, "Begin the Beguine," July 24, 1938

Bebop / Modern Jazz

The small bands of the Swing Era helped set the stage for the next revolution in jazz. But the innovators of the mid- and late 1940s left behind many of the commercial trappings of their predecessors. They cared little about pleasing dancers or putting attractive singers in front of the band. Instead they prized instrumental prowess and improvisational skills. Above all, they wanted to broaden the vocabulary of jazz, and were willing to take chances to do so, even if that meant they would never achieve the crossover fame of a Goodman or Ellington. Fans started referring to this new, strident sound as *modern jazz*—with the implication that it was akin to the modern painting of a Picasso or the modern architecture of a Frank Lloyd Wright. With this kind of pedigree, the music was expected to shock (and sometimes even bewilder) the general public, and its practitioners did their best to oblige.

New listeners coming to this music for the first time will immediately feel the difference. First and foremost, they will notice the speed and virtuosity of the performances.

Not every song was played at a lightning pace, but the fast and frenetic numbers seemed to capture the essence of *bebop* (as this music came to be called; sometimes shortened further to the onomatopoeic *bop*)—a style that took no prisoners and made extreme demands on the performers as well as the audience. Indeed, few dared to dance to the boppers, and for the first time in the history of jazz, the fans of the music gained a reputation as rapt and respectful listeners who stayed seated and often even refrained from conversation while the performers were in session.

This music is complex, and it would be easy for an outsider to get lost in the technical nuances of the bebop revolution. But I would advise novices to put those factors aside when they first listen to modern jazz and to initially focus on the energy and exuberance of bop in full flight. For all its technical sophistication, modern jazz isn't a cold, clinical demonstration of musicological concepts. The bebop aesthetic is more akin to the jousting of medieval knights or some sort of daredevil exhibition of high-wire stunts. Before taking an analytical approach, you should immerse yourself in the sheer visceral intensity of these performances, which capture the ethos of extreme sports transferred to the realm of instrumental improvisation.

But, yes, there is also plenty to analyze here. And as you gain familiarity with this body of work, these aspects will become more obvious. The leading exponents of bebop— Charlie Parker, Dizzy Gillespie, Bud Powell, Thelonious

Monk, and their colleagues—had new ideas about jazz melody, phrasing, harmony, and rhythm. These were so startling that their music faced a backlash from other jazz musicians as well as from fans whose expectations had been shaped by the conventions of Swing Era dance bands.

Judging by the controversies, you might think that the beboppers abandoned all of the key elements of prewar jazz. But that was hardly the case. The instruments of jazz remained largely the same, with a rhythm section of piano, bass, drums, and sometimes guitar supporting the horn players—typically saxophonists, trumpeters, and occasionally trombonists. The song forms of modern jazz also tended to adhere to the twelve-bar, sixteen-bar, and thirty-two bar structures that were popular in the 1930s, and in some instances the bebop compositions adopted the exact same harmonic sequences that underpinned the hit tunes of an earlier day.

Almost everything else in the music was new and different. Melody lines and improvised phrases got longer, faster, and more intricate. They are often filled with color tones, chromatic notes that would cause a dissonance if held for more than a fraction of a second, but when used appropriately in the middle of a phrase impart a pleasing balance between tension and release. The syncopations of New Orleans and Chicago still have a role in modern jazz, but are not as prominent as they once were—in some instances, soloists fire off a steady stream of notes that stay on the beat for measures at a time, with off-beat accents serving only as an occasional spice. The accompanying rhythm section responds by reconfiguring the underlying pulse in exciting new ways. Bass players still tend to play on the beat, but with a much smoother delivery that rarely signals when one measure ends and the next begins.

Indeed, virtually every song in the bebop repertoire is in 4/4 time, but this underlying structure is now far less obvious to the uninitiated listener. The drummers of modern jazz are even more daring, embracing a more disjunctive, pointillistic sense of time, yet with an unrelenting intensity heightened by unexpected accents and interjections. Piano players, by this stage in the music's evolution, have mostly abandoned the strong rhythms of stride in favor of a more oblique style. Bop keyboardists rarely laid out an obvious beat and instead focused on providing occasional rhythmic accents in the background or serving up long, loping melodic lines in the foreground very similar to what the horn players were doing.

As this description makes clear, these innovations were collective in nature: every member of the band participates in the great leap forward. Yet jazz also becomes more individualistic during this period. More than ever, it is a heroic enterprise, and the leading soloists in the music are admired for their iconoclasm, their personalities, their uncompromising stances. This perspective changes the ethos of the music, with sometimes surprising results. When the 'lost recordings' of Charlie Parker, made by obsessive fan Dean

Benedetti, finally got rediscovered and released thirty-five years after the saxophonist's death, they only included Parker's alto solos. Benedetti had failed to record the rest of the performances, so only these snippets of songs survived. Current-day consumers no doubt find this cut-and-paste approach bizarre and disruptive to their listening experience, but it reflects the new tone of jazz in the modern era. The individual solo had always been important, but now the prowess of the soloist eclipsed almost everything else in the music. Devotees turned to Parker, Gillespie, and their peers, immersing themselves in the virtuosity and creative outpourings of the bebop craft, seeing these as more than just musical demonstrations, but also emblems of social rebellion and sources of personal transcendence.

We should hardly be surprised that music of this sort became associated with various facets of the counterculture. When the term "bebop" got mentioned in newspapers or magazines in the late 1940s and 1950s, it often came packaged with a snide pejorative attitude. Modern jazz was associated with beatniks and hipsters and others on the fringes of society. To some, the music even seemed dangerous, inspiring irreverence and perhaps even threatening public morality. Even as the art form continued to morph and evolve in later years, this sense that jazz was an underground movement persisted—and to a surprising extent it still affects the portrayal and perception of jazz and its performers in the current day.

BEBOP / MODERN JAZZ:
RECOMMENDED LISTENING

Dizzy Gillespie, "Hot House," May 11, 1945
Dizzy Gillespie, "Salt Peanuts," May 11, 1945
Thelonious Monk, "Epistrophy," July 2, 1948
Thelonious Monk, "'Round Midnight," November 21, 1947
Charlie Parker, "Donna Lee," May 8, 1947
Charlie Parker, "Ko-Ko," November 26, 1945
Charlie Parker, "Night in Tunisia," March 28, 1946
Bud Powell, "Cherokee," February 23, 1949
Bud Powell, "Un Poco Loco," May 1, 1951

Cool Jazz

Bebop never found a large commercial audience, but it did attract a cadre of sophisticated devotees while earning be-grudging respect from the general public as cutting-edge music, the newest new thing in jazz. This period of ascendancy came and went with surprising speed. No one could keep at the forefront of the jazz world for long during the Cold War years. Like newly crowned boxing champions, leaders of each succeeding movement had to face ambitious rivals, upstarts determined to assert their supremacy and knock everyone else down a peg.

Even before the close of the 1940s, a reaction against the bop ethos could be heard on both the East Coast and West Coast. In time, this movement got a name—'cool jazz.' The contrast with bebop could hardly be more striking. On the tracks from his 1949 and 1950 sessions, now known as the *Birth of the Cool*, trumpeter Miles Davis fronts a nine-piece ensemble that stands out for its shimmering instrumental textures, relaxed rhythms, and understated melodicism. The influence of classical composers, especially impressionists such as Debussy and Ravel, can be heard in this music, and the concert hall ambiance is furthered by the use of French horn and tuba alongside the more familiar jazz instruments. Yet the improvised solos are as surprising as the composed passages, displaying a restrained lyricism and emotional delicacy that boldly breaks away from the paradigms of swing and bop.

Few paid attention at the time, and Davis's nonet gave only a handful of performances before the individual members went their separate ways. But over the next several years, Davis and his former colleagues would bring the 'cool school' to the forefront of the jazz world. The leading cool jazz performers even attracted a crossover following, enjoying occasional radio hits and finding a receptive audience at college campuses and other settings where boppers seldom ventured.

In fact, you can trace most of the key developments in cool jazz during the 1950s and early 1960s back to the various alums of Davis's short-lived ensemble. Davis himself would rise to stardom over the course of the next decade, a period that culminated with the release of *Kind of Blue*, the biggest-selling mainstream jazz album of all time and a defining statement of the cool aesthetic. He also reunited with arranger Gil Evans, who played a key role in defining the sound of the *Birth of the Cool* band, on a series of high-profile projects, most notably *Miles Ahead* (1957), *Porgy & Bess* (1959), and *Sketches of Spain* (1960). Baritone saxophonist Gerry Mulligan, who also served as performer and arranger with the *Birth of the Cool* band, found success as a rising star, most notably in his West Coast quartet alongside trumpeter Chet Baker. John Lewis, the pianist with the Davis nonet, would do the same with his Modern Jazz Quartet, which refined a cerebral yet sweetly swinging breed of jazz chamber music. Gunther Schuller, who played French horn with the Davis band, went even further in mixing classical music and jazz. He served as visionary leader of a musical movement known as the Third Stream, which aimed at nothing less than a large-scale merging of the classical and jazz idioms into a new hybrid.

You can hear the connection to the earlier jazz tradition in many of the leading cool jazz artists. Stan Getz, the most successful of the cool school saxophonists, never hid his admiration for Lester Young, that stalwart of the Kansas City sound whose horn stylings now influenced a generation of younger players. Young's light, airy sound and gift for melodic improvisation was a departure from the norm back in the 1930s, but during the 1950s this now seemed like the perfect recipe for cool jazz crossover success. Other artists linked to the movement were even bolder, mixing in the cool aesthetic with a host of experimental techniques. Dave Brubeck, the most prominent of the many jazz artists affiliated with cool jazz on the West Coast, drew heavily on the techniques of modernist classical composers and played a key role in introducing unusual time signatures into jazz, most notably on his recording of "Take Five," which proved to everyone's surprise that a song in 5/4 could be a huge radio hit. But Brubeck's band never lost its ties to the cool movement, and that aesthetic was especially evident in the lyrical sax work of his longtime collaborator, altoist Paul Desmond, who composed this signature song.

During the early 1960s, the cool jazz revolution no longer seemed quite so revolutionary. Other, even bolder artists were pushing jazz in new directions. But the cool approach survived—even thrived—in unexpected ways, often by getting assimilated into other styles of music. You heard echoes of cool jazz in movie and television show themes, from *The Pink Panther* to the Charlie Brown TV specials. The bossa nova movement emerged as a huge fad on the airwaves, but few listeners realized that these Brazilian artists were influenced by the cool jazz albums that had been exported to South America. Even today, when you hear a jazz sax solo on a pop album or in some other unexpected setting, the music often draws on the innovations of the cool school pioneers. I was hardly surprised when Pulitzer Prize–winning classical composer John Adams released a saxophone concerto in 2013 that was eerily reminiscent of Stan Getz's 1961 *Focus* album. There is a very good reason for all this borrowing: the cool advocates created a style of jazz that was perfectly suited for blending and hybridization with other musical idioms. Even as the cool movement lost its luster in the jazz community, it lived on as part of the global genetic code of the commercial music industry.

COOL JAZZ: RECOMMENDED LISTENING

Chet Baker, "But Not for Me," February 15, 1954
Dave Brubeck and Paul Desmond, "You Go to My Head,"
    October 1952
Miles Davis and Gil Evans, "Blues for Pablo," May 23, 1957
Miles Davis, "Fran Dance," May 26, 1958
Miles Davis, "So What," March 2, 1959
Stan Getz, "Moonlight in Vermont," March 11, 1952
Modern Jazz Quartet, "Django," December 23, 1954
Gerry Mulligan and Chet Baker, "Line for Lyons,"
    September 2, 1952

Hard Bop

Many jazz fans simply refer to this style as the *Blue Note sound,* in deference to the record label most closely associated with the glory days of hard bop in the 1950s and 1960s.

That linkage isn't entirely fair: Blue Note Records also recorded traditional jazz by Sidney Bechet, boogie woogie by
Meade Lux Lewis, atonal jazz by Cecil Taylor, and works
of other artists of various lineages and predilections. But
when most fans hear the name Blue Note, the first thing
that comes to mind is usually one of the soulful and funky
small combo albums that redefined the parameters of modern jazz during the Eisenhower-Kennedy years. This was
the quintessential hot music to warm up Cold War ears.

As the name "hard bop" indicates, the leading performers in this new idiom learned from their bebop predecessors. But they also borrowed techniques from rhythm and
blues, gospel, and other styles of populist music. The resulting hybrid artfully mixed the sophistication of modern jazz
with a rough-and-tumble swagger, brash and bluesy, that
never let you forget this music's proletarian pedigree.

In my teens, I worked a hard-hat construction job and
met a cadre of fellow blue-collar laborers who—somewhat
to my surprise—had a taste for jazz. It was the soulful Blue
Note jazz that earned their allegiance. And for good reason:
the musicians themselves seemed also involved in demanding physical labor. You could see them working up a sweat
on the monochrome album covers that capture the ethos
of the music. Or in live performance: the preeminent hard
bop drummer Art Blakey would even show up for work as
bandleader dressed in overalls. When asked by a persnick-
ety audience member why he was attired for the gig in

working-class garb, Blakey was quick to retort: "Because I'm going to *work!*"

The melodies on the hard bop albums tended toward an insistent earthiness. These players could still take off in free flight, drawing on the same kind of intricate explorations we find in 1940s bebop, yet these baroque tendencies were frequently tempered by a soulful directness that eschewed frills and ornamentation. The rhythms were driving, played with a bite that reminded you that hard boppers were rebelling against the musing moods of cool jazz. But the rhythm sections in these bands also drew on danceable grooves that the modern jazz players of the 1940s had mostly avoided.

At its best, this music achieved an artful balance between the crowd-pleasing beats and the mandate, now embedded in the DNA of jazz, to morph and experiment. The hard boppers constantly looked outside the jazz idiom for new concepts they could adopt and adapt, with everything from mambo to the boogaloo finding its way into their music. Horace Silver sought inspiration in the Cape Verdean music he had learned from his father; Benny Golson composed "Blues March," which took the squarest beat and made it hip, and drummer Art Blakey brought it into hard bop band's repertoire; other Blue Note artists would push the envelope in various ways, from the cerebral funkiness of Herbie Hancock's mid-1960s releases to the oblique tone poems of Wayne Shorter's efforts during this same period. Much of the vitality of the hard bop idiom came from this constant dialogue with commercial and progressive currents from outside the jazz world.

Almost every hard bop performance featured a small combo, most typically piano, bass, and drums supporting a front line of between one and three horns. Sax and trumpet were an especially popular combination, but sometimes trombone got added to the mix. Yet an alternate formula built around Hammond organ, electric guitar, and tenor sax emerged as a popular variant, especially on the funkier jazz albums of the day. The music was almost entirely instrumental; although the melodies were often catchy and perfectly suited for singing, hard bop bands rarely hired vocalists. Many a fan, however, probably sang or hummed along to the music, and in a few instances a lyric might be grafted onto a melody after the fact—as the Buckinghams did with Cannonball Adderley's "Mercy, Mercy, Mercy."

Yet even without a singer, hard bop songs could enjoy mainstream success and find their way onto the charts alongside the popular rock and R&B hits of the day. Lee Morgan's "The Sidewinder," for example, was a surprise jukebox success in 1965, and Herbie Hancock's "Watermelon Man" was a top-ten hit for Afro-Cuban percussionist Mongo Santamaría in 1963. This crossover appeal continues in the current music scene, when hard bop licks and beats from back in the day are sampled and recycled by hip-hoppers and DJs.

HARD BOP / SOUL JAZZ: RECOMMENDED LISTENING

Cannonball Adderley, "Mercy, Mercy, Mercy," October 20, 1966

Art Blakey, "Moanin'," October 30, 1958

Clifford Brown and Max Roach, "Sandu," February 25, 1955

Art Farmer and Benny Golson, "Killer Joe," February 6–10, 1960

Herbie Hancock, "Cantaloupe Island," June 17, 1964

Lee Morgan, "The Sidewinder," December 21, 1963

Wayne Shorter, "Witch Hunt," December 24, 1964

Horace Silver, "Señor Blues," November 10, 1956

Jimmy Smith, "Midnight Special," April 25, 1960

Avant-Garde / Free Jazz

The pace of change in the jazz world accelerated during the middle decades of the twentieth century, almost as if music were a kind of science that could only justify itself by relentlessly superseding old paradigms and establishing new ones. The mandate of the day was to overcome obstacles, burst through barriers, rewrite the laws of jazz, or even throw the whole rule book out the window. By the late 1950s, the final barriers in jazz were the music's continued allegiance to metrical rhythms, phrasing within the constraints of the chord, and maintenance of a tonal center. But within a few short years, these last precepts were challenged and rejected. In a very real sense, anything now seemed possible within the jazz idiom, the music's scope limited only by the imagination and bravado of its most visionary performers. This avant-garde movement, dubbed "free" jazz, asserted its proud independence from all traditions that had previously imparted structure to the music and ensured its commercial viability. For its most fervent advocates, the music was not just another style but the inescapable destiny of the art form—or, in the words of one of the most influential albums of the day: *The Shape of Jazz to Come.*

Yet in other regards, the comparison to science is misleading. I suspect many listeners find it difficult to enjoy free jazz because they approach the music weighed down with too much conceptual baggage. They try to assimilate the music by placing it in an intellectual and ideological framework, and the musicians themselves have often encouraged this by the theory-laden ways in which they discuss the avant-garde movement. But sometimes the best approach is an emotional one, almost the same way you would surrender yourself to the energy of a hard rock performance or the adrenalin rush of an action movie. Cecil Taylor, one of the leaders of this movement, once made a revealing aside. "To feel," he explained, "is the most terrifying thing in this society."[4] We should approach avant-garde jazz with his injunction in mind, striving to feel rather than merely intellectualize the music.

You can always come back and analyze it later. But in your first exposure, try to forget the term paper terminology and cocktail party high culture conversation jargon, and open yourself up to the experiential quality of the music. Instead of listening closely for the individual notes, immerse yourself in the sound. Instead of counting beats or seeking out structural landmarks, ride the flow of the performance. Consider it as a kind of aural landscape, a wild one where the symmetries of streets and borders are no longer there to guide you, but which is all the more exciting for their absence.

In an odd way, this music returns to the African roots of jazz. The avant-garde movement reversed the decades-long process of codifying jazz in terms of Western systems of scales and discrete notes. With the more transgressive works in the avant-garde jazz pantheon—Ornette Coleman's *Free Jazz*, John Coltrane's *Ascension*, Albert Ayler's *Spiritual Unity*—the music simply resists codification and assimilation into scale-based frameworks. Even if you wanted to transcribe the performance and capture it on music paper, you couldn't do it with conventional Western notation. By treating an Albert Ayler solo as a sequence of notes, you would leave out too much, replacing the saxophonist's impassioned testifying with a false and unreliable testimony, a kind of musicological perjury.

Once you have started to feel the music, you can move on to identifying the ways these practitioners deconstruct the metrical symmetries of previous jazz styles, at times refusing to embrace any sustained rhythmical structure, yet somehow imparting a fierce forward momentum to the music that echoes the 'swing' of their predecessors. Hear how they expand the conception of notes and phrases, crossing over the borderline between music and undifferentiated sound or even noise. Even when these artists played with conventional chord changes—as almost all of them did at some point in their careers—they invariably pushed against the limits of consonance, moving into dissonance and almost inevitably into an astringent atonality, where the comforting harmonic resolutions of everyday music are no longer an option. In their most extreme endeavors, all preexisting constraints were abandoned, the result a delirious mixture of anarchy and transcendence that took the essential spontaneity of the jazz ethos and pushed it to its absolute limits.

Yet the avant-garde movement wasn't all *Sturm und Drang*. These same iconoclasts also proved capable of emotional nuance, even a dialogue with highbrow and commercial styles of the day. The same Ornette Coleman who pulled out all the stops with *Free Jazz* could also achieve the pensive melancholy of "Lonely Woman," the austerity of "Morning Song," and the funkiness of *Dancing in Your Head*. Cecil Taylor collaborated with ballet stars Mikhail

Baryshnikov and Heather Watts, and even engaged in duets with Kansas City veteran Mary Lou Williams. The Art Ensemble of Chicago brought many elements of performance art and world music into their work, which covered the full range from swaggering energy jazz to pointillistic sound collages. The avant-garde advocates may have fallen short of their implicit goal of defining the *final* stage of jazz history, the sound of the future—in fact, other "newest of the new thing" approaches would emerge in their wake—but they laid the groundwork for their successors by the very boldness with which they questioned aural hierarchies and disrupted conventional ways.

AVANT-GARDE / FREE JAZZ: RECOMMENDED LISTENING

Art Ensemble of Chicago, "A Jackson in Your House,"
June 23, 1969
Albert Ayler, "The Wizard," July 10, 1964
Ornette Coleman, "Free Jazz," December 21, 1960
Ornette Coleman, "Lonely Woman," May 22, 1959
John Coltrane, "Ascension (Edition II)," June 28, 1965
John Coltrane, "Selflessness," October 14, 1965
Eric Dolphy, "Out to Lunch," February 25, 1964
Cecil Taylor, "Abyss," July 2, 1974
Cecil Taylor, "Conquistador," October 6, 1966

Jazz / Rock Fusion

By the 1960s, jazz had earned an unprecedented degree of legitimacy and cultural cachet. Once excluded from college campuses, it now formed part of the official curriculum in ivied halls. The government even enlisted jazz musicians as unofficial diplomats, smoothing over tense situations in potential trouble spots with this now respectable cultural export. And when Duke Ellington celebrated his seventieth birthday at the White House in 1969, no one found it incongruous or alarming. Jazz, once shunned by 'respectable' folks, had joined their ranks.*

Yet these successes could hardly hide the disturbing fact that jazz had gradually lost much of its mainstream audience during the years following World War II. The very steps that had validated the aesthetic ambitions of jazz practitioners—notably their willingness to experiment and push at boundaries—had reduced the music's commercial prospects. Like impoverished members of nobility fallen on hard times, the Dukes and Counts of jazz were honored and praised, but no longer could they rely on a host of loyal subjects to attend their public appearances and buy their albums. The listening public, especially those under the age of thirty, had moved on to other styles, other artists.

---

*Duke Ellington wasn't the first member of his family to visit the White House. His father had done occasional menial work there as a hired hand during the Warren Harding administration. But that merely makes the later hospitality extended to the son as fêted guest all the sweeter.

But the rise of rock also presented a rare opportunity for a reinvigorated dialogue between jazz and commercial music. Miles Davis, who had started the cool school rebellion two decades before, played a decisive role in fusing jazz and rock with his seminal 1970 release *Bitches Brew*, which quickly sold a half million units—around ten times the demand for a typical jazz hit record during this period. Others soon jumped on the fusion bandwagon, but the most prominent artists were those who had apprenticed with Davis, including keyboardists Herbie Hancock and Chick Corea, guitarist John McLaughlin, and saxophonist Wayne Shorter.

This makeover extended to the instruments on the bandstand. Electric guitar had been part of the jazz scene since the late 1930s, but now it achieved an unprecedented prominence in the fusion bands—defining the raw and heavily amplified aural textures of the style and also serving as a major solo voice, playing a role akin to that of sax and trumpet in earlier ensembles. Electric bass, previously a rarity in jazz, increasingly replaced the traditional upright bass in the most popular bands of the day. The piano also required a technology upgrade, at least in the context of the fusion idiom. Its role was now assumed by a host of plugged-in keyboards, including the Fender Rhodes electric piano, various synthesizers, and the Hammond B-3 organ, previously a staple in soul jazz combos but now used for its wailing, rock-oriented sounds. Technologies for tone manipulation had been part of jazz from the beginning, when New Orleans horn players relied on mutes to distort their notes, but now a new range of tools entered the music, from wah-wah pedals to Echoplex. When the hot fusion bands came to town, the stage often resembled a mad scientist's laboratory, packed with strange and wonderful equipment of futuristic appearance and unknown powers.

This music was often dismissed by purists as a sellout at the time of its initial release, and some feared that jazz was, for the first time in its history, backing away from its mandate to move forward, to experiment, to embrace the most progressive currents. And, true, in some instances, tired commercial formulas got overworked, and the music was dumbed down. But the best fusion work was innovative and expanded the jazz vocabulary at a time when—especially after late-stage John Coltrane and Albert Ayler—many concluded that everything that could be done in jazz had been done.

So don't approach this music expecting a slick commercial sound, akin to the smooth jazz that emerged later. Instead, listen for the wide range of creative stances at play, and hear the full scope of influences that came into jazz at this juncture. Miles Davis's *Bitches Brew*, the defining album of the movement, is a case in point. This expansive, free-flowing music defies almost every rule of commercial music. Instead of tight, hook-filled tunes suitable for radio airplay, Davis delivered long, mood-shifting rock-ish tone poems—tracks of ten minutes, or twenty minutes, or longer—that resist formulas. Or, perhaps it's more accurate to say he created new ones previously unknown in the jazz world. How strange that this prickly, unapologetic music should be viewed as a bid for crossover success. Yes, Davis achieved mega-sales, but you will seek in vain for artistic compromise on these tracks.

And then compare this exciting venture with the world-music-meets-electric-jazz work of John McLaughlin's Mahavishnu Orchestra, where the influence of everything from Indian ragas to prog rock can be heard. Or with the funk and strut of Herbie Hancock's Headhunters band from this same period. Or Chick Corea's mix of Latin, pop, and jazz into a seamless hybrid sound with his Return to Forever ensemble. Or explore the expansive sound collages of Weather Report, or the jazz-oriented albums released by Frank Zappa during this period, or the electrified, meter-mashing music of bandleader Don Ellis. All of these ensembles dipped deeply into the popular music of the day, but always from an expansive jazz perspective, surprising listeners with the vitality of the end results.

In time, the balance between commercial and aesthetic considerations became tilted too much toward the former. The exploratory attitude of early fusion gradually got supplanted by the slick formulas of smooth jazz. The rise of smooth jazz radio during the 1980s accelerated this process, as more and more labels and bands tried to match their sound with the tightly defined formats imposed by station program directors. But during the first blossoming of the fusion sound, during the late 1960s and 1970s, the movement stirred up the music world, broadened the vocabulary of improvised music, and showed that jazz could still benefit from give-and-take with popular styles.

JAZZ / ROCK FUSION:
RECOMMENDED LISTENING

Chick Corea, "Spain," October 1972
Miles Davis, "Pharaoh's Dance," August 21, 1969
Miles Davis, "Right Off," April 7, 1970
Don Ellis, "Indian Lady," September 19, 1967
Herbie Hancock, "Chameleon," September 1973
John McLaughlin, "The Noonward Race," August 14, 1971
Steely Dan, "Aja," 1977
Weather Report, "Birdland," 1977
Frank Zappa, "Peaches en Regalia," July–August 1969

Classical / World Music / Jazz Fusion

Just as 1950s and 1960s jazz fans learned to refer to hard bop as the "Blue Note sound," so would later listeners call this subsequent movement the "ECM sound." The name comes from ECM Records, a Munich-based label founded in 1969 by Manfred Eicher, whose vision and aesthetic tastes have exerted a marked influence on jazz during the last half century. The designation, as with Blue Note, is an oversimplification: Eicher and his company have championed a wide range of musical styles, and eventually expanded their focus beyond the confines of jazz. Even so, the congruent musical values of many of the leading artists associated with ECM justifies giving the lion's share of credit to this cadre of improvisers for the *other* type of fusion, which came to the forefront of the jazz world in the 1970s.

Even before the launch of ECM, many jazz artists looked for inspiration outside the dominant genres of African American and commercial music. As we have seen, jazz itself was a hybrid style of music from the moment of its birth, drawing on a grab bag of influences and turning them into something shockingly new. This ability to digest and absorb new sonic ingredients has persisted throughout its history. Gunther Schuller proposed, back in 1957, that a merging of jazz and classical music into what he called a 'Third Stream' offered a promising path for future composers and improvisers. Even earlier, leading jazz artists had looked to non-US performance styles, especially from Latin America, as a way of broadening the scope of the music. But these initiatives only hinted at the full potential of the hybrid approach, as it would evolve in the 1970s and after.

The boldness of this music comes across in many ways, not the least in what its practitioners decide to *leave out* of the performance. Long stretches might go by without any swing-oriented syncopation or bent blues notes, longtime calling cards of the jazz trade. In their place, listeners might encounter a bittersweet Chopinesque melody, or a quasi-medieval drone, or a jittery ostinato, an austere diatonic hymn, or a host of other attitudes, techniques, and devices that, just a few years before, might have seemed incompatible with the mandates of jazz. I recall, during my college days, playing a Keith Jarrett solo piano piece for a retired Stanford professor who prided himself on his deep knowledge of music. He immediately assumed that this improvised piece was a classical composition, but he struggled to figure out which previous century or decade might have spawned it. Wrong on both counts! But I could hardly blame him for the confusion. Jarrett and his contemporaries seemed determined to digest and assimilate the riches of all epochs and traditions in the long history of music. Sometimes I felt that, if I listened long enough, almost every musical meme, whether familiar or archaic, jazzy or otherwise, would eventually have its moment in this ever-shifting aural kaleidoscope.

Yet what this description leaves out is the remarkable holistic unity of these performances. You might think that music of this sort, with so many sources of influence and inspiration, would sound like a pastiche. How could this hodge-podge of sounds of such disparate lineages cohere into a seamless work of art, without jarring transitions or anachronistic juxtapositions? Nevertheless, the end result is anything but a mishmash. Indeed, one of the defining qualities of the ECM sound (and the music of fellow travelers on other labels) is the confidence with which the old threads are woven together, with no loose strands left hanging. The listener forgets about where the music originated or how different raw materials were manipulated into this new shape. I chafe a little at the audacity of the label's motto—"the most beautiful sound next to silence"— but the phrase does capture the sense of an aesthetic vision so self-contained that it cannot be reduced to a list of antecedents or ingredients.

The cross-cultural hybridization at play here was assisted, to no small degree, by the varied geographies and personal histories involved in the creation of the music. Jazz had spread beyond the United States at a very early stage, and Europe had spawned a handful of genuine innovators, even back in the 1930s, when guitarist Django Reinhardt enlivened Paris nightlife with his distinctive take on improvisation. But the new global and classical fusion of the 1970s represented a quasi–United Nations movement within the jazz idiom. Most of these recordings were made outside the United States, and a significant percentage of the performers came from Europe, South America, or Asia. In some instances, a single band might include representatives from several regions or continents.

I should note that, at this late stage in the evolution of jazz, different styles increasingly coexist and overlap. An artist such as guitarist Pat Metheny can be assigned to the jazz-rock fusion camp or the ECM school, or even move into the avant-garde on his *Song X* album with Ornette Coleman. Pianist Keith Jarrett might perform most of a concert obeying the strict rules of tonal-centered music, but then dip into atonal free jazz for shorter or longer interludes, or even compose his own orchestral works. For the acute listener, the rules of the game change accordingly, and much of the joy of experiencing this music arrives when you stop worrying about the stylistic guideposts so prominent in earlier manifestations of jazz, and focus instead on the ways jazz during this period sought to move beyond narrow labels and predictable formulas.

CLASSICAL / WORLD MUSIC / JAZZ FUSION: RECOMMENDED LISTENING

Jan Garbarek, "Dansere," November 1975

Egberto Gismonti, "Baião Malandro," November 1977

Dave Holland, "Conference of the Birds," November 30, 1972

Keith Jarrett, "In Front," November 10, 1971

Keith Jarrett, "The Journey Home," 1977

Keith Jarrett, "Solo Concert: Bremen, Germany, Part I," July 12, 1973

Pat Metheny, "Minuano," 1987

Jim Pepper, "Witchi-Tai-To," 1983

Enrico Rava, "The Pilgrim and the Stars," June 1975

Ralph Towner and Gary Burton, "Icarus," July 26–27, 1974

Postmodernism and Neoclassical Jazz

Jazz musicians who came of age in the final decades of the twentieth century were exposed, in varying degrees, to all of the styles described above. The jazz world had turned into a type of musical buffet, in which every taste and curiosity could be satisfied. Even as new styles emerged, the older ones continued to flourish, and each generation of jazz performers seemed increasingly skillful at moving from one to another. In the days of bop and swing, improvisers almost always kept loyal to the idiom and vocabulary of their formative years: a New Orleans trad player didn't evolve into a bebopper, just as beboppers rarely turned into avant-garde atonalists. Styles coexisted but, like wary nations, kept their borders well defended. Starting in the 1980s, a different attitude prevailed. "Why choose?" asked many members of the up-and-coming generation. Why couldn't a musician range freely through these riches, mixing and matching as passing moods dictated?

To some extent, the jazz world was simply following along with the broader currents of postmodernism sweeping through other art forms. In almost every creative field, a sense of end-of-history ennui had set in. Perhaps (as some feared and others relished) no more new frontiers remained to be conquered—at a minimum, the old linear model of art forms progressing like quasi-sciences no longer seemed quite so convincing—but artists could still achieve a certain freshness and piquancy if they were sufficiently bold in manipulating and realigning the bits and pieces of the various traditions inherited from the past. Old bric-a-brac could be dusted off and reconfigured into new mosaics, perhaps infused with new meanings, especially when approached with a sufficiently ironic or provocative attitude.

Consider the career of saxophonist John Zorn, who during a five-year period in the 1980s issued recordings devoted to the movie scores of Ennio Morricone (*The Big Gundown*, 1985); the hard bop stylings of pianist Sonny Clark (*Voodoo*, 1986); game music driven by cue cards and rules (*Cobra*, 1987); chamber and combo pieces inspired by a noir aesthetic (*Spillane*, 1987); and the avant-garde jazz of Ornette Coleman mixed with punk rock (*Spy vs. Spy*, 1989); among other projects. Zorn was an extreme case, but many of his contemporaries instinctively understood the charm of a style-without-a-style, a perspective on jazz that allowed them so much freedom to deconstruct and recombine all the music memes in the global jukebox. These were the first gene splicers of jazz, and the DNA they were manipulating came from the assorted legacies of previous generations of innovators.

Much of this music was deliberately playful and jesting, and you are advised to approach it with that in mind. But a more earnest approach to earlier musical styles emerged at almost the same moment on the jazz scene and, despite its obvious differences from the pastiche approach of Zorn & Co., shares enough similarities with it to warrant consideration as part of the same tectonic shift in the art form.

Music critic Gary Giddins has assigned the label "neo-classicism" to this attitude, which came to the forefront of the jazz world during the 1980s, and the comparison with neoclassicism in other art forms, which have also wrestled with ways of balancing responsibilities to the past against the mandate to push ahead into the future, is an especially apt one.

Wynton Marsalis stands out as the most famous musician associated with this approach, which consciously embraced the jazz idiom as a historical repository of cultural signifiers and viewed the next step in the art form's evolution as an ongoing dialogue between old and new. Yet Marsalis was only one of many jazz players of the period who felt that the paradigm of constant revolution that had mesmerized improvisers for decades needed to be tempered by active efforts, both artistic and institutional, to celebrate and revitalize what they had inherited from their predecessors. This mandate seemed all the more urgent given the growing indifference of the power brokers in the music industry to the preceding eighty years of jazz history.

I am focused on the music, so I won't dwell on the institutional ramifications of this shift. Others have written copiously, and with vehemence, on the pros and cons of this change in the jazz infrastructure, and you can find no shortage of opinions with a search engine query. Go at it, if you are so inclined.[5] Put briefly, the art form needed to find support from philanthropists, academia, and nonprofit organizations to weather this downturn in jazz's economic prospects, and despite fits and starts, and more than a few dissenting opinions, this transition took place during the last two decades of the century. But the music also changed and a timeline charting, for example, the stylistic evolution of Wynton Marsalis over this same period would show him moving from disruptor to consolidator, from fiery iconoclast to eloquent traditionalist. He, too, became a gene splicer of jazz memes.

At first glance, this music may seem a world away from the zany postmodernism of Zorn and others like him. And, yes, the retro jazz players who embraced traditional techniques at this juncture had little patience for the irony, or sometimes outright flippancy, of the postmodernists. But both groups shared an obsessive concern with the vocabularies of the past and sought to make them fresh and relevant to a new generation. Those approaching jazz of this sort for the first time shouldn't be surprised if they hear echoes of some (or all) of the previous styles, discussed above, in both camps.

Given the complex lineages informing jazz of this type, audiences can adopt a range of listening strategies. Improvised music during the closing years of the twentieth century could serve a pedagogical purpose—not surprising, perhaps, given the expansion of jazz programs in educational institutions during this same period. You can hear the whole history of jazz hiding inside this music, and songs can even be treated as museum exhibits. Or you can analyze the aesthetic attitudes embodied in these works, which cover the full spectrum from tongue-in-cheek frivolity to extreme gravitas. Indeed, no period in jazz invites more acute philosophical speculation and debate. Or you can simply enjoy the fast-changing soundscapes; many of these songs pack the wallop of a theme park ride. Despite the heated internal arguments this music spurred in the jazz world at the time of its ascendancy, the clash and clang of styles and agendas was fun and invigorating. Best of all, try out all of these listening stances, and see how they impact your assessment of the music.

POSTMODERNISM AND NEOCLASSICAL: RECOMMENDED LISTENING

Don Byron, "Wedding Dance," September 1992

Bill Frisell, "Live to Tell," March 1992

Wynton Marsalis, "A Foggy Day," 1986

Wynton Marsalis, "The Majesty of the Blues (The Puhee-man Strut)," October 1988

Marcus Robert, "Jungle Blues," 1990

Henry Threadgill, "Black Hands Bejeweled," September 20, 1987

World Saxophone Quartet, "Night Train," November 1988

John Zorn, "The Big Gundown," 1984–1985

SIX

A Closer Look at Some Jazz Innovators

S TUDIES OF JAZZ OFTEN READ LIKE A LITANY OF LARGER-THAN-LIFE characters, towering figures who remade the art form in their own image. They are described in whispery, reverent terms with a lot of emphasis on colorful anecdotes about their eccentricities and out-of-control behavior. I'll admit it makes for an interesting story.

Yet jazz commentary has perhaps focused too much on arrest records, drug habits, and unconventional lifestyles. Maybe I should have warned you on page 1 that if you want to hear about Louis Armstrong's devotion to marijuana and Swiss Kriss, or Charlie Parker's incarceration in a mental institution, this is not the book for you. I don't dismiss these tales as totally irrelevant—indeed, I've come to the conclusion that an art form built on improvisation and spontaneous decisions will attract a disproportionate

percentage of unpredictable characters into the ranks of
its practitioners. But I feel even more passionately that the
reason why we still care about these individuals is their
artistry, not their addictions or capricious behavior off the
bandstand. For this reason, we began our exploration of
jazz with a clear focus on the key ingredients in the music
itself, and gradually expanded our perspective to encom-
pass stylistic and cultural contexts within which the specific
artists made their contributions. These factors are essential
starting points for grasping the significance of any particular performer. You don't get Neil Armstrong without a
space program. Nor do we encounter a Louis Armstrong
(no relation) without the assistance of a certain sociocul-
tural ecosystem.

Yet we've all been swept away by a touch of hero worship. Back when I was in college, I had photos of jazz musicians taped all over my dorm room walls—probably fifty
or more images, some actual glossy prints, others just pages
torn from magazines. My wife wouldn't allow this type of
interior decorating in our current home, but I'd still hang
publicity photos on the wall if it wouldn't create such a fuss
on the domestic front. I'm still a 'fan' today, and I don't feel
the slightest hesitation in using that word. And now that we
have studied the principles, origins, and evolution of jazz, I
can indulge some of this obsession with the heroes of jazz.
But keeping true to this book's mission, I will continue to
focus on musical matters and listening strategies. We owe it
to these musicians to put that ahead of, say, their rap sheets

or broken marriages; but, even more to the point, this is the best way to learn about jazz.

Below I focus on a handful of artists who not only had a decisive impact on the jazz scene of their own eras, but whose legacies have stood the test of time. They continue to influence and inspire, and their surviving works shape the ongoing jazz dialogue. Certainly this short list of greats does not represent a full roster of innovators—a large number of musicians have made substantial contributions to the idiom—but the listening skills honed in appraising these seminal figures can be applied to other artists in turn. My goal is not to treat exhaustively all the twists and turns in the jazz world over the last century, but to open up your ears and add to your appreciation of the music. I believe that this goal is often better realized by focusing intensively on a small number of artists, immersing ourselves in their works, than by hurriedly sampling the efforts of a long litany of players.

Let's start with perhaps the biggest hero of them all, at least in my personal jazz hall of fame.

Louis Armstrong

The summer between my junior and senior years in college I pursued an unusual musical experiment over a period of two weeks. If I hadn't invested that time, I don't believe I would have ever really understood, beyond a superficial level, the essence of Louis Armstrong's contribution to jazz.

You probably think that my experiment involved close study of his music, but you would be dead wrong.

In fact, my experiment required that I *stop* listening to Armstrong's recordings. Even more, I refused to listen to any musician who had been influenced by Armstrong or any jazz made after his classic recordings of the mid- and late 1920s, the so-called Hot Fives and Hot Sevens. For two weeks, I listened only to jazz made *before* Louis Armstrong developed his mature style. This limited my options considerably. When I wanted to hear music, I could only choose from the recordings of the Original Dixieland Jazz Band (1917), Wilbur Sweatman's Original Jazz Band (1918), Kid Ory's Sunshine Orchestra (1922), King Oliver's Creole Band (1923), and a handful of other pioneers of early jazz.

Day after day, I immersed myself in these tracks by the very first jazz bands. I adjusted my ears to the scope and stylistic devices of the music, and gradually felt at home with the sound of the creators of New Orleans jazz. And then, after two weeks, I returned to Louis Armstrong's breakthrough recordings made between 1925 and 1928. I was hardly prepared for what I now heard. What a revelation . . . indeed, what a shock! Everything about Armstrong's conception seemed to propel the art form ahead by light years. I now realized, with spine-tingling certainty, that these classic Hot Fives and Hot Sevens, so often considered old-fashioned examples of traditional jazz, represented the most progressive, forward-looking music of their day.

At this juncture in the art form's history, Armstrong literally introduced hundreds of new phrases into the jazz vocabulary. But far more striking than the notes—even those flamboyant high ones—was Armstrong's virtuosity with syncopation and accents. Jazz possessed a rhythmic vitality from the start, but Armstrong clearly grasped the potential of syncopated phrasing at a level far beyond his predecessors. It's as if we have moved, in a single, inspired step-change, from Euclid's geometry to Newton's calculus. But the complexity was balanced by a warmth and endearing human quality, epitomized in Armstrong's rich, full tone, which allowed his quasi-avant-garde progressivism to flourish simultaneously as party music for the Jazz Age.

This is how to listen to Louis Armstrong: Put out of your mind any notion that you are *exploring the tradition* or *revisiting the roots* or *paying tribute to your great grandpa's generation*, or any such hare-brained idea. This is bold, unapologetic music, and by treating it as an antiquated museum piece you are doing it a disservice. We need to recalibrate our perceptions and experience this music as part of the same spirit that, during the 1920s, also produced the masterworks of Joyce, Woolf, and Proust.

That's hard to do, and Armstrong himself is to blame. He was just too successful. He was simply too influential. All of his innovations were studied and borrowed by others, and not just by horn players—composers and arrangers, singers, pianists, Tin Pan Alley tunesmiths, the whole creative class in the music industry learned from his example. By the early 1930s, his personal musical vocabulary was showing up everywhere. He couldn't patent or copyright it but merely gifted it to posterity. As a result, you need to make the effort to purge your ears of these borrowings in order to appreciate how much Armstrong changed the art form. By my measure, he had the biggest impact of anyone, and number 2 isn't even close.

Once you have learned to listen to Armstrong in this manner, you can hone in on his other achievements. He was a consummate entertainer, an extraordinary singer (applying to his vocal work many of the same breakthroughs that set his trumpet work apart from his peers), a charismatic celebrity, and, in time, a movie star and cultural ambassador. By all means, check out these various aspects of the Armstrong persona. But if you've kept your ears open and listen perspicaciously, you won't forget that this larger-than-life pop culture figure was, first and foremost, a musical innovator of the highest rank.

Where to Start with Louis Armstrong: This is an easy call. If they ever make a list of the seven wonders of the ancient jazz world, the Hot Fives and Hot Sevens get two of the slots. But these recordings, made before Armstrong's twenty-seventh birthday, are merely the opening highlights in a long career filled with vital tracks. It's well worth your time to check out the recordings Armstrong made at the end of the 1920s and during the early 1930s, when he was at the peak of his powers. Then move on to sample the highlights of his mid- and late career—for example, *Louis Armstrong Plays W. C. Handy* (1954), *The Great Chicago Concert* (1956), and *Ella and Louis* (1956). Finish up with his late-career hit singles "Hello, Dolly!" and "What a Wonderful World."

Coleman Hawkins

Music fans today can hardly imagine how disruptive the saxophone was during the early days of jazz. Even decades after the sax had taken over the bandstand, many New Orleans purists objected to its baneful presence. And the instrument had other marks against it. The sax was not an accepted symphonic instrument—the American Symphony Orchestra League even issued a formal prohibition of the horn during the 1920s. It was loud and lowbrow and perhaps even morally dangerous. I've heard stories, perhaps apocryphal, of radio stations refusing to play sax music on the Sabbath, fearing its corrupting influence on impressionable young souls. But there's little doubt that Pope Pius X had the sax in mind when, at the dawn of the twentieth century, he instructed the clergy to avoid instruments "that may give reasonable cause for disgust and scandal."[1]

The saxophone not only survived this backlash, but would eventually take its place as the defining sound of jazz. And most of the credit for this stunning turnabout goes to a single musician: Coleman Hawkins. Born in St. Louis in 1904, Hawkins learned cello and piano as a youngster, but turned to the saxophone at age nine. At that stage, Hawkins was playing the C-melody saxophone, rarely heard in jazz nowadays, and was still doing so when he made his first recording with blues singer Mamie Smith in May 1922. But that summer he switched to the tenor sax, a rarity on the bandstand during that era. With few role models to draw on, Hawkins had to define and develop an authentic jazz voice on his horn, and he did so with so much success that, almost a century later, the key building blocks of his approach still exert an influence on horn players. And not just in the jazz sphere: you will often hear saxophonists in rock, pop, and R&B bands who channel Hawkins's persona in their on-stage stylings.

When you listen to Hawkins's music for the first time, start by focusing on the tone. You can tell even within a few notes that Hawkins didn't aim to create a smooth symphonic sound. The notes are muscular and declamatory, although avoiding the extremes of harshness. His aesthetic decisions are driven by a commitment to channeling his personality into the horn, to stand out rather than to adapt to the hive mind of the formal orchestra. It's hardly a coincidence that, even in the glory days of the big band, Hawkins made his most memorable recordings with small combos, where his horn was the star attraction. His vision as an artist led him to precisely that destiny. As part of this conception, Hawkins conveyed an intangible but discernible sense of confidence, or perhaps what we call today *self-actualization*—an assertiveness that gives his improvisations a forward momentum that his predecessors on reed instruments (primarily clarinetists and C-melody saxophonists) rarely matched.

Now turn your attention to the phrases, the intricate web of notes that Hawkins spins from the bell of his horn. Hawkins represented a new breed of jazz player. His musical instincts were guided by considerable formal training, perhaps some of it at Washburn College in Topeka, where he claimed to have been a student (although his name does not appear in its files). In any event, Hawkins soon gained a reputation for his advanced grasp of harmony and ability to navigate through the most complex songs. In an art form dominated, at that juncture in history, by players with strong ears and sometimes very little technical knowledge—an extreme example is cornetist Bix Beiderbecke, twenty months older than Hawkins, who struggled with reading music until the end of his life—this pioneering tenor saxophonist brought to bear a more overtly analytical approach to the music. It's easy to miss this cerebral aspect of Hawk's playing, given the emotional force of his improvisations, but it's at the core of his contribution to jazz, and helps explain how he managed to adapt more successfully than his peers to the modern jazz movement of the 1940s.

Both of these elements, the sound and the phrasing, jump out at the listener in Hawkins's most famous performance, his 1939 recording of "Body and Soul." If you ranked sax improvisations from the 1930s on the basis of intellectual rigor and sheer complexity, this track contends for top spot. But Hawkins's "Body and Soul" was also a hit record, and I suspect that few of the bar patrons who put a nickel in the jukebox to hear this horn performance were following the subtle harmonic implications of the passing phrases. Yet they responded to the passion of the music, which evoked a kind of macho romanticism that demanded their attention. Like many of my favorite jazz performances, this track operates at two levels, making a visceral appeal to casual fans while offering hidden riches to those willing to take the time and trouble to listen deeply. One such audience member was future tenor legend Sonny Rollins, who, at the age of ten, heard Hawkins's "Body and Soul" playing from a jukebox at the Big Apple Bar on the corner of 135th Street and Seventh Avenue in Harlem. "A light went off in my head," Rollins would recall years later. "If he could personalize a popular song like that without lyrics, any song was possible if you had that intellectual capacity."[2]

Hawkins would continue to make recordings for another thirty years after this unexpected crossover hit. During this period, he constantly pushed himself outside of the usual comfort zone for early jazz stars. He subsequently appeared on recordings with Thelonious Monk, Duke Ellington, Dizzy Gillespie, John Coltrane, Oscar Peterson, Sonny Rollins, Paul Bley, and other artists of diverse stylistic allegiances. In his later days, he shared the stage at the Monterey Jazz Festival with avant-gardist Ornette Coleman, experimented with Brazilian bossa nova, and saw his trademarked licks show up on rock albums. I can't imagine any other jazz artist who had been recording back in the early 1920s, when Hawk made his first sides, surviving in the tumultuous 1960s with such composure, let alone thriving in so many unfamiliar settings. "I got a record of you playing tenor in 1904," bebopper Sonny Stitt joked with Hawkins during a late career road tour—a slight exaggeration, perhaps, but somehow it seemed fitting.[3] Wasn't Coleman Hawkins the father of jazz sax? Hadn't he written the rule book for the horn? Yet here he was, comfortably adjusting to every new twist and turn in the music.

You might be best served, as a listening strategy, to forget that Hawkins was acknowledged as the "father of the saxophone." Think of him instead as the eternal student of the horn, as the discoverer of a new world who never stopped exploring its further reaches. Immerse yourself in Hawkins's recordings from different stages of his career, and see how he is constantly probing, adapting, learning. In defining the sound of the tenor sax in jazz, he drew on its potential for brash, virile statements, but when the occasion warranted he could make it into the gentlest of instruments, a moody accompaniment for lovers. He came to prominence through his knack for long, elaborate phrases, but if the setting demanded, he could shift to a blues moan or whispery asides. He could be teasing or soothing, melodic or experimental, old fashioned or newfangled, or find some constructive midpoint between these various extremes. When you grasp this protean aspect of Hawkins's artistry, you will realize that he influenced not only the sound of jazz but also its attitude of openness and malleability. Indeed, his role in this regard may be just as great as his impact on improvisation techniques.

Where to Start with Coleman Hawkins: Go straight to Hawkins's 1939 recording of "Body and Soul," which has been studied and imitated by generations of jazz players. To put this track in context, sample some of his earlier recordings—for example, Hawkins's work on "It's the Talk of the Town" with Fletcher Henderson from 1933 or "Emaline" with Benny Goodman from the following year. Then focus on Hawkins's seminal work from the late 1930s and early 1940s, when he was the most influential saxophonist in jazz—the December 1943 session with Eddie Heywood, Oscar Pettiford, and Shelly Manne, and his February 1944 tracks with Dizzy Gillespie warrant your closest attention. His solo recording of "Picasso" (1948) was a milestone moment in jazz, showing that the saxophone could stand alone as an unaccompanied instrument. Finish by enjoying at least one or two of his late-career albums. You might want to consider his projects with Ben Webster (1957), Henry "Red" Allen (1957–1958), Red Garland (1959), Duke Ellington (1962), or Sonny Rollins (1963).

Duke Ellington

Duke Ellington is the emblematic figure who sums up, better than anyone, the guiding concerns of this book. If I need to support my view that listening skills ought to serve as the foundation for any approach to jazz, I merely turn to his precedent. "Yes, I am the world's greatest listener," he announced in his autobiography. He made the same point in other settings, reinforcing the centrality of listening to the jazz experience—even to the creative process underpinning the art form. "The only thing I do in music is listen," he told critic Ralph Gleason in a television interview in 1960. Then he added, "Listening is the most important thing in music."[4]

These weren't empty words. Ellington lived up to them, and achieved a rare degree of artistry by putting them into practice day after day. He was a commercial bandleader and a major force in the jazz world from the mid-1920s to the early 1970s, and had to deal with the realities of the music business almost every day of his life—and did so with deftness and extraordinary success. He was a talented hit maker and a key force in establishing swing jazz as the popular music of America in the years leading up to World War II, but he was also an ambitious composer who refused to be restricted by the expectations of the marketplace. Here too he succeeded, gloriously and against the odds. Nowadays you will hear Duke Ellington's name mentioned on lists of great American composers, honored alongside Aaron Copland, Charles Ives, George Gershwin, John Philip Sousa, and other illustrious figures. Rightly so! But his music differs from these others in a profound way. Almost every important piece Ellington ever composed was written to showcase the key skills he heard in his band members. Music almost became a platform for Ellington's management of human resources, and the end result was something you simply didn't encounter in any other jazz ensemble, then or now.

Billy Strayhorn, Ellington's closest collaborator, explained this essential part of the music in an interview with Bill Coss: "In Ellington's band, a man more or less owns his solos until he leaves. Sometimes we shift solos, but usually they're too individual to shift. You never replace a man; you get another man. When you have a new man, you write him a new thing. It's certainly one of the reasons why the music is so distinctive. It's based on characteristics." Strayhorn might have gone further and emphasized that Ellington raised the level of difficulty in this approach by seeking out players with highly stylized, almost eccentric sounds. For example, no band relied more on mutes to create personal horn textures. When forced to choose a new member for the orchestra (a rare occasion in this ensemble of long-tenured professionals), Ellington put little stock in the virtuosity and technical parameters other bandleaders cherished. He would rather hire a player with technical limitations but who had a distinctive tone or engaging musical personality. From these disparate pieces of sound, Ellington constructed masterpiece after masterpiece, building compositions in a quirky manner taught in no music conservatory but extraordinarily powerful when practiced with such subtlety and vision. And when you think about it, the Ellington way makes perfect sense: How can you go wrong if the notes are tailored to the strengths of the performers? Ellington wasn't boasting, merely explaining his creative process when, toward the end of his life, he wrote, "Here I am fifty years later, still getting cats to come out of bed, so that I can listen to them."[5]

So let's return the favor, and listen to Duke Ellington with the same focus and respect that he gave his band. If we do this, what do we hear? Well, perhaps we should start with what earliest fans of this band heard and praised, namely its exoticism and distinctive sound textures. The press frequently used the term "jungle music" to describe the sound of the early Ellington band. The phrase is filled with unfortunate overtones, and we would do best to avoid it. But the underlying musical ingredients that gave rise to this description warrant our attention. Ellington's idiosyncratic aural textures jump out at you in his band's recordings, even on tracks from the 1920s such as "East St. Louis Toodle-Oo" and "Black and Tan Fantasy." From the start, Ellington's music sounded mysterious and alluring, to both the casual fan and highly trained listeners, and would continue to do so for the duration of his career. "You know," conductor and composer Andre Previn once admitted, "Stan Kenton can stand in front of a thousand fiddles and a thousand brass and make a dramatic gesture and every studio arranger can nod his head and say, 'Oh, yes, that's done like this.' But Duke merely lifts his fingers, three horns make a sound, and I don't know what it is."[6]

Perhaps this music did sound primal and uninhibited to the band's fans at the Cotton Club—a ritzy all-white nightclub in the midst of Harlem where Ellington presided over the musical entertainment—during the 1920s and 1930s. But if they probed more deeply into the structure of Ellington's compositions, they would encounter an almost geometrically austere formalism that contrasts sharply with the surface energy of the performances. No jazz composer of his day—or in the long history of African American vernacular music—was more ambitious in breaking free of the prevalent twelve- and thirty-two-bar song forms and exploring the many possible ways of combining themes, chords, and interludes within the context of a three-minute (or occasionally a longer) recording. This is a subject worthy of a doctoral dissertation. But if you look back at the discussion of Ellington's "Sepia Panorama" in Chapter 3, you will get some sense of the formal complexities at play in his music. If you took the time to study the construction of fifty or so of Ellington's tracks, and compared them with other recordings of his day, you would see over and over this composer's unique skill in conveying a sense of an uninhibited party on the surface level but underpinning it with sober calculation in the music's inner workings. In fact, I suspect that a few readers will decide, after their initial sampling of Ellington's work, that they want to make the time for this deeper immersion in his work.

Last yet hardly least, you listen to Duke Ellington's oeuvre for more reasons than just Ellington. No other artist

mentioned in these pages was more obsessed with show-
casing the distinctive contributions of colleagues in song
after song. This started with the compositions themselves,
often drawn from ideas created by band members or developed, in small or large part, by Ellington's frequent collaborator Billy Strayhorn. And when these works showed up
on a record or the bandstand, they were channeled into the
musical personae of the familiar, beloved characters of the
orchestra. To love Ellington's music is also to cherish these
individuals—for example, alto saxophonist Johnny Hodges,
who joined the band in 1928 and, except for a brief time
apart in the early 1950s, was still performing with the ensemble a few days before his death in 1970. Or baritone
saxophonist Harry Carney, who spent forty-five years in
the Ellington band. Other performers clocked in twenty or
more years on the road with the Duke. Much of my joy in
listening to this music comes from the thrill of hearing a
Johnny Hodges glissando, or how Bubber Miley could turn
his trumpet into a horn of plenty with only the help of a
mere plunger mute—pretty much the same tool you use to
unclog a stubborn drain. Pay these individuals the attention
they deserve. Don't focus just on what Ellington gives, but
also on what he takes, and marvel at the way he was energized by his employees. You can learn a lot from that kind
of give-and-take, and many of those lessons can be applied
far beyond the realm of music.

Indeed, in my twenties I learned about this unheralded
side of Ellington's legacy from an unlikely source. In my

first job out of college, I took a position with the Boston Consulting Group, a high-profile professional firm that offered expensive advice to Fortune 500 CEOs. (I wasn't the only musical outlier on the payroll—future R&B star John Legend was also a consultant with BCG around that same time.) Here I discovered to my surprise that the consultancy recommended Duke Ellington to clients as a source of managerial wisdom. Ellington's executive skills could be compared to Benny Goodman's, and the contrast was striking. Goodman was a perfectionist who was rarely pleased with the musicians he hired, and they burnt out on his intensity, many leaving the band after only a short stint. Ellington's orchestra thrived, in contrast, because the boss didn't demand perfection, and instead built everything in the ensemble's repertoire on the demonstrated strengths of his personnel. The team flourished, and many members stayed on for decades. I suspect that this approach to leadership could work in any environment, but its success in the jazz field is beyond debate. No ensemble in the history of the music can match the Ellington orchestra's half century of constant productivity and high artistry.[7]

Where to Start with Duke Ellington: Duke Ellington's recording career spanned a half century, and every period in the band's evolution produced vital music. But I will admit that my favorite era of Ellingtonia is the late 1930s and early 1940s. I am chastened not only by the conceptual boldness of the scores and great solos from the band, but also by the stunning fact that Duke was at his peak of popularity during this stint. Somehow he managed to expand his artistic ambitions even as he was producing jukebox and radio hits. Some readers will drop their jaws at the correlation, but perhaps the best comparison here is with the evolution of the Beatles during the 1960s, a remarkable period of advancement in which each new record seemed to open up new panoramas. Of course, the two bands are very different, but both somehow managed to break rules and experiment with radical new ways of constructing songs, yet still bring a mass audience along for the ride. In Ellington's case, I suggest you start with the 1940–1941 ensemble (sometimes called the Blanton-Webster band), and then sample a few other tracks from this era. I especially like the live recording in Fargo, North Dakota (1940), and strongly recommend Ellington's ambitious *Black, Brown & Beige* suite, performed at Carnegie Hall in 1943. You also need to hear some of the early Ellington tracks, for example the great Bubber Miley feature numbers "Black and Tan Fantasy," "East St. Louis Toodle-oo," and "The Mooche." I will also admit a partiality for the *Masterpieces by Ellington* album from 1950, his *Harlem* tone poem from 1951, and *Piano Reflections* from 1953. If you're ready for more, move on to the live recording at Newport (1956), *A Concert of Sacred Music* (1966), and the later suites, perhaps *Such Sweet Thunder* (inspired by Shakespeare) or *Far East Suite*.

Billie Holiday

We have now arrived at Billie Holiday, who will force you
to put aside the analytical mindset that helps guide the 'appreciation' (a sad word, that one; perhaps music appreciation teachers should replace it with something a little less
tepid?) of so many other artists. Maybe someday we will
have mathematical tools to deconstruct the microtonal nuances and rhythmic freedom of her singing. There must be
a kind of science behind what Billie Holiday achieved. I
don't doubt it. But for the time being, we are best advised
to approach her music through its emotional valence.

In fact, the novice listener may even have an advantage
over the trained academics. In approaching Billie Holiday,
there are no substitute chord changes to admire, no intricate licks awash in chromatic trickery, no surprising mod-
ulations or pyrotechnics in the upper register. I won't go
so far as to say that Holiday isn't a virtuoso. She is, but of a
different sort, more qualitative and psychological, and not
at all flashy. I see her more as a diagnostician of the soul,
whose music reaches into those vulnerabilities and emotional risks that many of us avoid or actively repress.

My focus here is on musical style more than biography.
But Holiday herself invited us to see these two as intimately
connected, at least in her case. Her 1956 autobiography
Lady Sings the Blues, written with the help of collaborator
William Dufty, was the first tell–all jazz memoir. We are
all familiar with frank public confessions nowadays, but

commercial entertainers simply didn't share *these* kinds of details back in the Eisenhower era. Here's the opening, to give you a taste: "Mom and Pop were just a couple of kids when they got married. He was eighteen, she was sixteen, and I was three." Holiday goes on to tell of abuse, addiction, prostitution, and other travails, but also to relate the story of her rise to fame during the 1930s as one of the most admired singers in jazz. I'm not convinced that hardships made her a better vocalist, but I don't doubt that Holiday's willingness to reveal them publicly, without the slightest tinge of self-pity, gives us some insight into a key component of her artistry. She was doing something similar, an unapologetic exposure, every time she stepped onto the bandstand or into a recording studio.[8]

Here again, the listener needs to respond in kind. Holiday invites each of us into a one-on-one relationship. This is not an idle claim or another example of critic hyperbole. From a precise historical standpoint, Billie Holiday represents the culmination of a series of changes that turned popular singing in America into a quest for intimacy and personal contact with the performer. This started with a technological innovation, namely the introduction of microphones and electrical amplification into popular music during the 1920s. For the first time, vocalists no longer needed to bellow and shout to reach the back rows; instead they could adopt a conversational stance or even coo and whisper to the audience. Bing Crosby and the crooners of the Jazz Age understood the new potential these technologies offered, and in response created a different way of singing. But Billie Holiday completed the task begun by these pioneers. More than any singer of her day, she showed how a jazz performer could strip away all the frills and mannerisms of the bandstand entertainer and create an illusion of direct rapport with the listener.

My advice to you could hardly be simpler. When listening to Billie Holiday, open yourself up to this connection. Later you can start to analyze, if you wish, but most of this analysis will probably center on the ways she subverts the slickness and demonstrative postures of your *American Idol* type of singer. Yes, Billie Holiday was a master of her craft, and what she achieved did involve technical skills. But at its foundation, it also required a poise and confidence to open herself up to this deep self-exposure for her audience. This kind of honesty doesn't go out of style the way musical gimmicks and fads do; so don't be surprised if this singer from a now distant era hits you with more immediacy than the vaunted pop sensations of the current day.

Where to Start with Billie Holiday: Holiday's recordings from the late 1930s and early 1940s, especially the tracks with saxophonist Lester Young, are essential listening—and not just for jazz fans. If you want to understand the evolution of modern vocal styles of any sort, or the development of American music in the twentieth century, you need to grapple with these performances. You can start out with "All of Me," "I Can't Get Started," and "Mean to

Me," but every track from this period is deserving of your attention, even the alternate takes (initially unreleased but now available, and worth the effort to find). By the close of this period, Holiday was already redefining her craft, most noticeably by recording "Strange Fruit," which daringly broached the subject of racial violence and lynchings on a commercial record. You should check out her 1939 recording of this work, and also sample some of the torch songs that served as her trademark pieces during the 1940s, such as "Lover Man" and "Good Morning Heartache." Holiday's voice had deteriorated by the 1950s, but even her late recordings are emotionally riveting—for example, the tracks recorded for producer Norman Granz in 1956 and 1957. Cap off your Holiday excursion by going to YouTube to watch the clip of her 1957 television rendition of "Fine and Mellow" for CBS, which I rank as my favorite jazz moment on film.

Charlie Parker

Charlie Parker holds a special place in my own development as a musician—and as a listener to music. During my formative years, I immersed myself in his recordings with the fervor of an acolyte seeking admission into a secret sect. I listened to his tracks at full speed and later at half speed. I tracked down rare bootlegs and compared them with the studio recordings. I studied transcriptions and made notes in the margin. I scrutinized the ways he built tension and release into his elaborate phrases and tried to formulate the rules implicit in these techniques.

But here's the strangest part of this story. I never had much interest in imitating Parker's style. I was very conscious of myself as part of a later generation of jazz musicians. Parker had died before I was born, and the key building blocks of my own approach to jazz came from musical currents that arose a quarter of a century after his seminal bebop recordings first appeared. Yet I still recognized a kind of perfection in Parker's improvisations that deserved the closest consideration. Perhaps "reverence" isn't too extreme a word to use in this regard. Probably the only other artist to inspire me to a similar degree was Johann Sebastian Bach—and in both cases, the era and style of the music seemed irrelevant. I was drawn to the almost Platonic ideal of mathematical precision married to emotional intensity in the work of these artists. Learning what made them tick served as a kind of musical calisthenics that, I hoped, would strengthen my mind, ears, and (ultimately) fingers, even as my own stylistic predilections took me down much different paths.

Parker had this impact on many others, especially during his lifetime. He came of age in Kansas City when it was the epicenter of a new style of bluesy jazz marked by its relaxed swing and streamlined 4/4 pulse. Parker mastered this idiom, but by the time he started making waves at Harlem jam sessions in the early 1940s, he had added a host of original techniques, distinguished by their intellectual weight and demonstrative virtuosity, to his arsenal. Many of the breakthroughs of the emerging bebop sound came directly from the bell of his horn, and though this new style never matched the widespread popularity of the Swing Era big bands, musicians took notice. Few of the older players could adapt to the demands of this new idiom, but the most adventurous younger musicians embraced bebop as the revolutionary sound of their generation and Parker as their generalissimo.

After the fact and in my own haphazard way, I identified with these acolytes, but realized that I could never match the loyalty of the most devoted of them—for example, Parker follower Dean Benedetti, for whom the term *follower* is more than just a metaphor. He literally pursued Parker from gig to gig, bringing a portable recording device with him to capture the stray improvisations of his mentor and master. (He followed Parker in less salubrious ways, too, succumbing to the same heroin addiction, which led to Benedetti's death at the age of thirty-four years and six months—the exact duration of Parker's life.) I could never match that degree of self-sublimation in another musician, yet I well understood how Parker's alluring artistry could tempt others into a kind of unquestioning discipleship.

How should you approach this body of work? I am assuming that you don't have years to devote to apprenticeship, in the manner of a Dean Benedetti. And the intricacies of Parker's music can be difficult to unravel—no, not the virtuosity, which will jump out and impress even the most casual listener. But there's more than sheer speed at the heart of his artistic vision, and the fireworks on the surface perhaps make it even harder to grasp many of the innovations at play in his music. But I have a solution to this, an approach for outsiders that I know works with newcomers to bebop. This is, I am convinced, the fastest way to get inside modern jazz.

I want you to sing along with the music.

I can already hear murmurs of dissent. Some of you are insisting that you are tone deaf and can't sing. Okay, you are allowed to hum or whistle or snort or whatever. Just try to internalize what Parker is playing on the horn, if only for a few measures, and join in by contributing your own approximation. You can start with the simpler stuff. Just focus on the melody, not the improvised solos (move on to those later, if you dare!). The melody to "Now's the Time," a twelve-bar blues, is not too daunting. "Billie's Bounce" is a little harder but still within the scope of a newbie. If you listen to the melody a half dozen times, you should be able to start 'performing' it along with Parker. "Moose the Mooche" and "Blues for Alice" will be harder, and "Confirmation" tougher still. But when you start vocalizing these melodies, you will be immersed in the essence of the bebop sound. You will *feel* the rhythmic structure of the phrases; you will internalize the chromaticism and cadences even if you have no notion of the technical rules that guide them. This will give you a deep sense of Parker's contributions to the jazz vocabulary. I've seen it happen with students and know it works.

You will probably also surprise yourself with how much you enjoy this approach to music. (And it works for other artists, not just Charlie Parker.) I find it deeply satisfying to vocalize in tandem with a great jazz performance, and I suspect you will too. Even if you stumble or are out of tune, you will gain insights into the music that are much harder to reach via quiet, passive listening.

Before we leave Charlie Parker behind, let me offer a few additional suggestions on how to approach his music. It's so easy to get lost in the maze-like structures of his bebop virtuosity that you might not realize the less extroverted elements of his playing. He was an incomparable interpreter of ballads—just as skilled at very slow numbers as he was at the barn-burning tempos for which he is more famous. In fact, he played popular tunes such as "Embraceable You" and "Don't Blame Me" at a slower beat than any of his peers, and helped to establish the very relaxed approach to these kinds of songs that is now widespread among improvisers. Listen to these tracks, and enjoy Parker's ability to infuse his elaborate phraseology with a heartfelt romanticism. He wasn't just a clinical avant-gardist, hell-bent on revolution, but also a consolidator of everything that had preceded him in the jazz tradition. For this same reason, you should also give particular attention to his blues performances, where you can hear how deep his roots go—his 1948 recording of "Parker's Mood" for the Savoy label ranks among the finest blues tracks in twentieth-century music, but there are a number of other fine examples in his oeuvre.

Where to Start with Charlie Parker: Start by focusing on Parker's recordings from 1945 to 1948. This extraordinary period encompasses Parker's stellar February and May 1945 tracks with Dizzy Gillespie, his seminal sides for the Savoy label, and the very influential recordings for Dial. A number of live recordings were also made during these years, and though many of them suffer from mediocre (or sometimes abysmal) sound quality, the best of these performances are well worth hearing. I would highlight the Town Hall recording from June 1945 and the Jazz at the Philharmonic concerts from 1946. You should also sample Parker's later recordings, now available on the Verve label. Parker's well-known tracks with string orchestra could have been much better if they had featured less saccharine arrangements, but they are still important milestones in the history of modern jazz. (Parker's personal favorite among his tracks was his 1949 version of "Just Friends" with strings.) I also recommend his June 1950 session with Dizzy Gillespie and Thelonious Monk, and his January 1951 date with Miles Davis. You could spend many a profitable hour listening to the later live recordings, but the best of them is the May 1953 performance at Massey Hall. This music has sometimes been described as the "greatest jazz concert ever," and though I would shy away from such a definite pronouncement, it's clearly required listening for serious jazz fans.

Thelonious Monk

In discussions of the rise of bebop, pianist Thelonious Monk is typically listed as one of the key innovators. Thus you might jump to the conclusion that his musical style was roughly similar to Charlie Parker's, perhaps even that they relied on the same phrases and rhythms, maybe even played the same tunes or frequently shared the bandstand. But lists are often misleading, especially so in the case of Thelonious Monk, who is best heard on his own terms rather than as a member of an artistic movement.

Monk certainly presided over the birth of bop and influenced its evolution, but his music is even more striking for the ways it subverted the formulas of the era. Monk rarely played at the ultra-fast tempos associated with bebop. His solos were almost completely free from the familiar licks and cadences of his contemporaries. Instead of the byzantine, free-flowing improvisations of his fellow modernists, Monk constructed his solos on crisp harmonic textures, rhythmic disjunctions, and a host of melodic devices of his own invention. And when it came to repertoire, he usually preferred to play his own compositions, while his peers preferred otherwise. (This changed over time, with many of his pieces gaining acceptance as jazz standards— but the mainstreaming of Monk's music took place, for the most part, after the pianist's death in 1982.) In short, the entertainment media may have dubbed Thelonious Monk as the "high priest of bop," but for many years it seemed as if his ministry had just one true believer, the artist himself, while few others could even grasp the peculiar quirky commandments of his sect.

You may have already heard that Monk's music is difficult, and perhaps my description so far adds to that impression. I won't deny that his style does present difficulties for other performers who hope to emulate it—partly because they may need to unlearn techniques they have relied on in other jazz settings. But for the listener who comes with open ears, the situation is much different. Many of his melodies are very hummable, and a few even possess a childlike simplicity not entirely dissimilar to a nursery song, although typically with some surprising or off-centered element added to the mix. And few jazz artists of any era are so easy to identify as Monk, whose stylistic tendencies jump out at the listener in almost every note he plays. Just listen to a few tracks, and you will feel that you could pick out Monk in a blindfold test. Keep on listening for a few hours, and your ears will start to recalibrate their expectations to the dimensions of his musical world. You will hear the humor in his performances, the conversational quality in his phrases and interjections, and the sense of delight in musical creation that permeates his oeuvre.

Let me emphasize the last point. Spontaneous creativity is an essential element in jazz. The most memorable moments in my many years of listening to jazz have come when a kind of telepathic communication of this spontaneity has moved beyond the bandstand into the audience. At a certain juncture in the music, everyone feels the vibe. The soloist—or maybe even the entire group—has tapped into some special energy; a quasi-divine spark of inspiration has lifted the music to a new level. Something different is happening that night, something that has *never* happened before. Maybe you even look at the other patrons and make eye contact—are you feeling what I'm feeling?—and they look back with that same expression. But this only happens when the musicians themselves have broken away from the formulaic or conventional, have entered what psychologist Mihaly Csikszentmihalyi calls the *flow state*,[9] perhaps with bravery or even better with a kind of innocent purity, a joyous confidence that whole new continents are awaiting exploration. I get that sense from Monk, even when just listening to a record. He seems completely open, without prejudice or preconception, to the full possibility of music. He operates in a kind of constant flow state in which aural doors, closed to others, open magically at his slightest gesture. And even those who merely listen can feel this, if they adjust their wavelength to his.

Note also Monk's economy of means through this whole process. I sometimes imagine a taxi meter device attached to each musician's instrument, counting every passing note, measuring who can say the most with the least expenditure of tones. Monk would win that contest. He will take you all the way across town on just spare change. There are no wasted gestures here, and even the pauses and hesitations are essential parts of the finished product. There is a greatness of omission that permeates Monk's music. More than any other jazz artist, Monk teaches us that an artist's style is like a sailing ship: those who make the most progress are often the most ruthless in throwing excess baggage overboard. Even novice listeners can hear it, but this is one aspect of Monk's approach that they might appreciate more after comparing his work with that of his peers. Jazz is a prolix art form, and its towering achievements almost always have something excessive about them. Monk not only resisted this tendency but overturned it. It's still a joy to hear and just as subversive now as it was back in the 1940s.

Where to Start with Thelonious Monk: Begin your exploration of Monk's music with his recordings for the Riverside label from the late 1950s. These present his best-known compositions in a wide range of settings: with his working bands, joined by guest artists, and as a solo pianist. It's hard to pick and choose among these riches, but I especially like the solo projects (*Thelonious Himself* and *Thelonious Alone in San Francisco*), his tracks with John Coltrane, and the *Brilliant Corners* album with Sonny Rollins. For a more in-depth listening experience, you can compare these with Monk's earlier recordings of many of these same compositions for the Blue Note label. The later Monk recordings for the Columbia label hold fewer surprises in

repertoire and accompanists, but there are many outstanding tracks here. Check out, for example, *Criss-Cross* (1963)
and *It's Monk's Time* (1964).

Miles Davis

I wish I could introduce this subject with one of those
clichés so often relied on by masters of ceremonies—something along the lines of "His accomplishments speak for
themselves" or "Here is a man who needs no introduction." The alternative is to attempt a short summary of a
career that resists compact summation. Davis constantly
reinvented his musical persona, and by the time most fans
had figured out what he was doing, he was already doing
something different. His early recordings find him playing
bebop alongside Charlie Parker, and at the end of his career he was advancing boldly into hip-hop. In between he
served as the leading exponent of cool jazz, invented modal
jazz, redefined the big band sound, and helped launch the
jazz-rock fusion revolution. If the twentieth century was
the most restless age in the history of music, Miles Davis
was its emblematic figure. Hell-bent on getting to the future before everyone else, Davis seemed willing to give up
everything in the process, even the jazz audience and expectations inspired by his own iconic work.

Perhaps you should approach Miles Davis the way you
might encounter a painter such as Pablo Picasso, who had
his "blue period" and "rose period" and other junctures of

stylistic reinvention.* Yet I am tempted to suggest the exact opposite. Instead of listening for the radical disjunctions in Davis's oeuvre, marvel at the extraordinary continuities, at the core virtues that emerge at every stage in this unprecedented musical evolution. In truth, Miles Davis was hardly a flexible, accommodating artist, and even as he appeared to adapt to changing styles and tastes, he never budged from his convictions. The starting point for an appreciation of Mr. Davis is to grasp what these were, and how they shaped almost every project he pursued.

I believe that the decisive moment in Davis's career came in the late 1940s, when he abandoned all attempts at matching the showy virtuosity of Dizzy Gillespie and the other leading beboppers. This would have been a courageous move at any juncture in music history, but especially in the midst of the modern jazz revolution, when speed and high-range hijinks were so prized. And for a trumpeter of unproven credentials such as Davis—who many thought wasn't ready for prime time when he had been hired by Charlie Parker, and was hardly a star when he went out on his own as a bandleader—this renunciation of flashy pyrotechnics could easily be interpreted as weakness, as an acceptance of the second rate. Yet over the next several years, Davis honed a range of other skills that would elevate his music for the rest of his career. At first these surprised the jazz world, most notably at the 1955 Newport Jazz Festival, where his rendition of

---

*One of the defining tracks of Davis's mid-career, composed to feature his distinctive talent by longtime collaborator Gil Evans, is appropriately entitled "Blues for Pablo."

"'Round Midnight" mesmerized the audience and helped Davis secure a contract with Columbia Records. But soon it became clear to anyone with ears that this moment of glory was no fluke. Put simply, there were some things that Miles Davis did better than anyone else, and achieved with such consummate skill that entire artistic movements would spring from his passing phases.

Everything started with what others might call Davis's unfailing instincts for melodic improvisation. And though I don't disagree with that description, it doesn't do full justice to what Davis brought to the bandstand. Let me put it differently: Davis somehow managed to make everything sound melodic—even a short, choppy phrase, or a single note, or (in the most extreme case) a mistake on the horn. Yes, as strange as it seems, even Davis's mistakes sound good to my ears. His way of shaping the phrase, or adding shades of texture to a tone, or altering it with a mute, or adjusting dynamics conveys a compelling human quality and sense of personality to every melodic line. This was true in 1955, and 1965, and 1975, and all the way to the end of his career.

These virtues stood out especially on slow numbers, and Davis could easily have built his entire career on his skill in interpreting romantic ballads.* Yet the same qualities also

---

*Davis was the unsurpassed master of such material in the 1950s and early 1960s but eventually left these tender love songs behind—just as he abandoned so many of his other signature numbers during his mercurial career. He commented on this in a cryptic but significant comment to pianist Keith Jarrett: "You know why I don't play ballads anymore? Because I love playing ballads so much." From Michael Ullman, "The Shimmer in the Motion of Things: An Interview with Keith Jarrett," *Fanfare* 16, no. 5 (May/June 1993): 114.

shaped his aesthetic vision on jaunty mid-tempo tunes and off-to-the-races energy pieces. No matter how fast the band was plunging ahead, Davis never sounded rushed or harried. Even on those mid-1960s albums with the rhythm section (pianist Herbie Hancock, bassist Ron Carter, and drummer Tony Williams) destroying the jazz equivalent of the space-time continuum around their middle-aged trumpeter boss, all at a Saturn V rocket booster level of energy, Davis is poised and in control, every phrase from his horn imposing its own gravity on the proceedings. Yes, this is what you can listen for, both to admire and to enjoy, on virtually every recording Davis made from each period in his post-1940s career.

But don't miss another core value, evident throughout Davis's oeuvre—one that's easy to overlook, despite its importance in his artistic success. Miles was known as a fierce individualist and demanding bandleader, and countless anecdotes testify to his prickly personality, yet the evidence of his musical output tells a very different story. No musician of his generation did a better job of blending in with the rest of the group, of creating coherent holistic statements that integrated the contributions of every member of the ensemble, many of them almost as assertive and demonstrative as their boss. You can hear this as early as his *Birth of the Cool* recordings from 1949 and 1950, but it is just as evident at every other phase of his evolution, from bebop to hip-hop, whether you are listening to *Kind of Blue* or *Bitches Brew* or any of his other masterworks. Commentators invariably recognized that Davis always surrounded himself with world-class musicians, and he earned credit as a formidable talent scout, but they rarely noted the beautiful karma at work in these ensembles. I am still not sure how Davis achieved this, but somehow he created coherent statements that were larger than the individual talents (enormous ones, I must add) surrounding him, even while every member was allowed to shine and contribute a personal statement, no one more magnificently than Miles himself. This must have been a tremendous balancing act, requiring constant care and nurturing—or perhaps taunts and badgering, who knows?—from the eminent Mr. Davis. In any event, the glorious end results live on for your delectation.

So, of course, you should savor the many stages in this artist's career, a progression that might be summed up by referring to the title of a famous Miles Davis album: *Seven Steps to Heaven*. Marvel at his ability to move from bebop to cool to impressionistic big band music to modes to hard bop to fusion to funk, and not only to adjust but to actually operate at the forefront of each movement. Pay attention to Davis's formidable reinvention of jazz trumpet, every half decade, more or less, and hear how this musician never ran out of new angles and bold moves. But don't miss the unity of purpose that encompasses each of these heavenly steps, or the force of personality that could take almost any new musical style and compel it to serve his personal vision.

Where to Start with Miles Davis: I really hate to pick and choose here. Almost everything Davis recorded between

1955 and 1970 rocks my world, and even outside this period I find many gems. So what do I do? I will cop out
and follow the crowd, recommending *Kind of Blue* (1959),
which has somehow become enshrined by pundits as the
definitive modern jazz album. I'm not sure I could defend
that claim, but this project is a masterpiece by any measure.
Yet you also need to sample Davis's collaborations with arranger Gil Evans, at a minimum *Miles Ahead* (1957), *Sketches
of Spain* (1960), and the early *Birth of the Cool* tracks (1949–
1950). Then move on to the mid-1960s band. *E.S.P.* (1965)
and *Miles Smiles* (1967) are outstanding examples, but you
might also want to explore the live performances from this
period, such as *In Europe* (1964) or the tracks recorded at the
Plugged Nickel in 1965, which find the Davis combo offering brash reinterpretations of the standard jazz repertoire.
Move on to the jazz-rock period: *Bitches Brew* (1970) is required listening, but also consider *Jack Johnson* (1971) and
On the Corner (1972). For dessert, listen to his late-career
cover versions of Michael Jackson ("Human Nature") and
Cyndi Lauper ("Time After Time").

John Coltrane

For a period of roughly forty years, jazz fans lived in the
Age of Heroes. Every few years a towering figure would
emerge, a world-changing alpha male—women were apparently excluded from consideration for this highest
rung in the hierarchy—who would redefine the rules of

improvisation and establish the zeitgeist with horn in hand. Louis Armstrong started this parade; his trumpet introduction to "West End Blues" from 1928 almost sounds like a fanfare for the hero's arrival on the bandstand. Later triumphant figures, from Coleman Hawkins to Charlie Parker to Miles Davis, reinforced the audience's expectation that this patriarchal dynasty would continue forever.

Yet it fizzled out. It's not that we lack jazz heroes in the present day. We face the opposite situation: we have too many of them. The diversity and pluralism of the jazz scene, good things for the most part, make it very difficult for any single artist to define the era or set the tone. I suspect jazz would be much more popular today if critics could give people a single name, a whispered hipster's talisman, as centerpiece and entry point into the scene. "Check out [fill in the hero's name here] and you will be one of the cool cats." Ah, it doesn't work that way, not anymore.

John Coltrane was the last of these world-beating heroes. In the years leading up to his death in 1967, when Coltrane succumbed to cancer at just age forty, jazz fans at the cutting edge awaited each of his albums as if it were a postcard from the future, signaling the start of the next new thing. Coltrane wore the mantle of these expectations with a rare degree of humility, focusing less on the acclaim and more on his own quest for self-improvement and advancement. For as long as possible, he had learned from the best—developing his talent, during the course of the 1950s, in the bands of Dizzy Gillespie, Thelonious Monk, and Miles Davis—and gradually drew acclaim as a major star in his own right. When he found himself at the forefront of jazz, he continued to practice, study, and evolve. At the dawn of the 1960s, a growing contingent of fans and critics lauded Coltrane as the latest heavyweight champion of jazz, the leader of what was fresh and new in the music; but he himself was too focused on getting better to bask in the glory.

This affects how we listen to Coltrane's music. Although audiences are tempted to treat any work from such an iconic figure as a finished masterpiece, I suspect that Coltrane himself would want us to view his music as a quest, as a work in progress. He was a seeker, as much in his personal life as in his music, and I doubt that his goal was to present posterity with a museum of perfectly realized musical statements. During the last decade of his life, he tried to do almost everything one could possibly do with a saxophone—inside the chords and out, within the framework of Western music and beyond, alongside old school musicians and with the most avant-garde players he could find. He understood both the potential and the risks of such an unrelenting incursion into the unknown. And even John Coltrane must have felt at times as if he were reaching the limits—a live recording at Temple University from late in his career finds him putting the sax aside, pounding on his chest, and vocalizing some ritualistic chant of his own inspired creed. Some of this work is accessible and easy to enjoy, even for jazz novices, but other parts of it will force you out of your comfort zone as a listener. Yet all of it was part of the quest, and the mindset you need to bring to it has to be different from the casual attitudes inculcated by our entertainment-oriented society. Listen to Coltrane as if you were going on a spiritual retreat or a five-day cleanse. Try, as much as possible, to approach his music with the same attitude of openness and discovery with which the artist created it.

With this openness as a starting point, you can apply a range of listening strategies to Coltrane's body of work. Those interested in the inner workings of music will find an inexhaustible supply of techniques inviting analysis. You could write a dissertation on just one facet—for example, his multitonic harmonic concepts (sometimes simply called "Coltrane changes" by jazz cats) or his modal scales. But even without the slightest knowledge of these topics, you can enjoy the virtuosity, the devilish speed of execution that critic Ira Gitler dubbed "sheets of sound." Yet you can just as easily look for the opposite, sublimation rather than showmanship. In fact, the whole body of Coltrane's work exhibits—like the artist himself—a surprising degree of self-control, a willingness to submerge the ego into something larger, whether via collaboration with a past master (listen to his project with Duke Ellington and relish the cross-generational give-and-take) or the evocation of some quasi-mystical state, celebrated in albums such as *A Love Supreme* and *Om*. (The latter includes chanted texts from the *Bhagavad Gita* and the *Tibetan Book of the Dead*.)

Or you can push it further, and try to participate in the transcendence. I don't routinely turn to jazz recordings for meditation music, but I don't doubt that Coltrane's work can be approached in this way. He even released an album called *Meditations*, although that particular disk will probably challenge your preconceptions about contemplative music. Or you can throw away the metaphysics and musicology and just savor Coltrane as a hot sax soloist, maybe the hottest of them all, a master improviser who could get into a horn battle with Sonny Rollins or Eric Dolphy, and match the best players note for note, phrase for phrase. Best of all, try out all of the above. Coltrane deserves that kind of flexibility and respect, and will reward you in turn for your open-mindedness.

Where to Start with John Coltrane: At first glance, Coltrane might seem easier to grasp than, say, Miles Davis. After all, Coltrane's best work spans roughly one decade. But he squeezed so much musical activity into this short period that the newcomer faces more than fifty albums to choose from, each one admired and acclaimed by devotees. So I will ruthlessly simplify the process for you and suggest two albums from each period. For early John Coltrane, when he still had strong ties to the hard bop tradition, I would recommend *Blue Train* and *Giant Steps*, both recorded in the late 1950s. For Coltrane's 1960s modal explorations, I recommend *My Favorite Things* and *A Love Supreme*. From his brief but inspired period of moody romanticism, I steer you to *Ballads* and *John Coltrane and Johnny Hartman*. For Coltrane's final plunge into free jazz, go to *Ascension* and *Meditations*. Start with the facet of this artist most aligned with your personal tastes, but then push yourself outside of your listening comfort zone.

Ornette Coleman

I've suggested repeatedly in these pages that the path to appreciating jazz is through the ears—by training and developing them—and not through digesting concepts and received opinion. Or, put differently, critics should aim to make their own role superfluous. This happens when informed listeners can hear what's happening in any performance and draw their own conclusions. The intense buzz that surrounded the rise to fame of saxophonist Ornette Coleman, who generated intense controversy in the jazz world during the late 1950s as the leader of the avant-garde, is a case in point. Few musicians have been dealt with so poorly by outside commentators. I can't think of another instance in jazz in which the written texts do so little justice to the body of work.

And this is true among both proponents and detractors. The latter were especially vehement during the early years of Coleman's career, when his ostracism almost amounted to quarantine from the jazz clubs of America. He was literally ordered off the bandstand by saxophonist Dexter Gordon. Miles Davis announced that Coleman was "screwed up inside."[10] Dizzy Gillespie denied that Coleman was even playing jazz. Drummer Max Roach allegedly punched Ornette in the mouth. This was the price Coleman paid as pioneer of avant-garde jazz during the 1950s, for daring to move outside the chord changes into atonality or frequently lingering in that middle zone between consonance and dissonance.

Yet Ornette Coleman was hardly better served by his advocates, whose praise often made his music seem daunting and impenetrable. The concept of the "future" was used so often in connection with his music—even the record labels pushed this notion, naming his albums *The Shape of Jazz to Come* and *Tomorrow Is the Question!*—that fans justifiably feared that their poor present-day noggins might be insufficient to the task of grappling with such cutting-edge fare before its time. This music was often marketed as if it were a time capsule sunk into the ground, awaiting some indeterminate future date when it could be dug up and reopened, finally sharing its riches with the world. So who can be surprised when many listeners decided to pass on those disks, leaving tomorrow's music for tomorrow's audience to decipher and critique?

Nor did Coleman help enlarge his fan base with his own pronouncements, which presented his artistic process as if it were driven by an arcane technology. He even devised a metaphysical-musicological platform for his music-making, described by Coleman as *harmolodics*, a quasi-science for initiates. But when he outlined the theory to outsiders, his hints and clues were as enigmatic as Zen koans, as esoteric as the higher teachings of the Rosicrucians.

You really ought to thrust all of this baggage aside when approaching Ornette Coleman. Instead, pay attention to the music—not what people have *said* about it. And if you go to the source and open your ears, what do you hear? First and foremost, Coleman's plaintive and often haunting sax sound will jump out at you; at least it does for me. It's a very human sound, and though it sometimes gets lost in the mix (for example, the famous *Free Jazz* album, praised for its radicalism, but in which Ornette's sax is often drowned out amid the two quartets playing simultaneously), I would highlight this personal and sometimes intimate tone as the magnetic center of this artist's appeal. You can't reduce it to theory and concepts, and those who want to approach Coleman with textbook in hand might even miss its beauty, but you shouldn't. The same is true of the bluesiness and sheer soulful passion in Coleman's music. These, too, can't be reduced to dogma and manifesto, and perhaps they even undercut the praise of those who elevated Ornette because of his revolutionary break with the past. But I am assuming that you want to listen to this music for enjoyment—that's true, isn't it?—and not just to impress cocktail party acquaintances with avant-garde name-dropping. So don't feel guilty about digging Coleman's roots and blues, and all the things he picked up gigging in R&B bands and soaked up from the gritty Texas and Southwest sax traditions that flourished during his formative years. Long before

Coleman took charge of the avant-garde, he was grooving in juke joints and roadhouses. So I'm hardly surprised that Coleman reinvented himself as a funk player at mid-career with his Prime Time band and showed up on recordings with Jerry Garcia of the Grateful Dead. A populist strain ran deep in this saxophonist's musical vision.

Only at this stage, after you have grasped these core elements of Ornette Coleman's DNA, do I give you permission to hear him as a badass musical revolutionary. Now put on that *Free Jazz* album, and blast the sound level to the max. Or throw a party, and put on that track where Coleman sets aside sax for violin and features his ten-year-old son on drums. Yes, he could be a desperado, and this is part of his charm. Certainly it's part of his historical significance. But never forget that Ornette Coleman wasn't a concept-driven composer akin to John Cage. His music is visceral and sweaty and in-the-moment; it's unpredictable and human, and coming out of the bell of his horn propelled by lung power and sheer determination. That's just another way of saying that he was a jazz musician, first and foremost. So come for the avant-garde credentials, and you can even drop Ornette Coleman's name at a cocktail party, I won't forbid it, but stay around for jazz. You might be surprised at what you hear.

Where to Start with Ornette Coleman: I would begin with the recordings Coleman made for the Atlantic label in 1959 and 1960. These weren't his first records, but they do represent his first mature statements in the context of his most important bands. On Coleman's bold and brilliant *The Shape of Jazz to Come*, a short thirty-eight-minute album from 1959, he is joined by trumpeter Don Cherry, bassist Charlie Haden, and drummer Billy Higgins— perfect accomplices for the altoist's reinvention of the jazz vocabulary. And before the end of the year, this same quartet returned to the studio to record *Change of the Century*, which reinforced Coleman's reputation as the leader of the jazz avant-garde. Only after sampling these works would I move on to *Free Jazz*, recorded in December 1960, which is a wickedly iconoclastic project and a defining moment in embracing noise and cacophony as tools in jazz self-expression. Coleman's subsequent albums for the Blue Note and Columbia labels aren't as well known but have many fine moments. Check out, for example, *At the Golden Circle Stockholm* (1965), *Science Fiction* (1971), and *Skies of America* (1972) to get a sense of the wide range of this artist's mid-career explorations. I am even more pleased by Coleman's funk phase, starting with *Dancing in Your Head* (1976), which I highly recommend. My favorites among his later albums are *Virgin Beauty* (1988) and Coleman's Pulitzer Prize–winning *Sound Grammar* (2005).

Further Observations

I have focused on just a handful of jazz innovators in this chapter, and I apologize if I have left out a favorite artist or recording. My goal, however, is not to offer a comprehensive guide to major jazz performers—that would take up an entire book on its own—but to help you expand the capacity of your ears and construct listening strategies that bring you closer to the essence of each artist's work. If you want to move on to a more comprehensive survey of jazz musicians and performances, I suggest you supplement this volume with more in-depth studies—for example, my books *The History of Jazz* and *The Jazz Standards*, or other comparable works on these subjects. The goal in these pages is more one of connoisseurship and discernment. Think of it as akin to learning how to taste and savor wines, which may be assisted by some specialized knowledge, but can still be practiced by those lacking a degree in viticulture. Music is much the same. In hot music as in pinot noirs and cabernets, this cultivation of an informed taste is really the foundation for advancing more deeply into the subject.

The term "connoisseur" has become degraded in recent years, and many avoid it, not without good reasons. Even when I hear the word, it summons up mental images of gentlemen in smoking jackets, sipping brandy and planning their bidding strategy for the next art auction at Sotheby's. And, it's true, connoisseurship has often been compromised by class and economic interests. But today, these distortions of wealth and power come less from snooty arts patrons and more from the institutional curation imposed on us by global entertainment corporations. They are the self-appointed connoisseurs of the current day and exert enormous influence over what music gets heard, shared, and praised. We do well to reclaim the concept of connoisseurship from these impersonal economic forces, and recognize an alternative hierarchy, in which knowledge and expertise trumps wealth and institutional power. For this reason, when I have tried to learn more about a style of music, I have sought out those who possess this expertise—typically people who have devoted decades to musical study and discernment. These are the true connoisseurs, and they are essential to a healthy music ecosystem. By the same token, this is the kind of connoisseurship we should all aspire to if we care about music, and no smoking jacket is required.

What other takeaways should you bring from this exploration of these jazz innovators? I hope that one lesson stands out: namely, the need to approach artists and styles on their own terms. As you have seen, the listening strategy can't be the same for every musician. I try to start each listening session with an open mind, and as the performance unfolds, I ask myself: What is this artist attempting to do? Some musicians are cerebral, others are passionate; some want to swing like crazy, while others are seeking a poetic romanticism; some are plunging into the future, while others want to preserve our legacy from the past. You can't judge all of these with the same rubric, and this is more than just a matter of fairness to the performers. More to the point, you will severely constrain your own listening pleasure if you fault New Orleans trad players for not sounding like beboppers or avant-gardists, or gripe that some introspective ECM ensemble doesn't swing like the Count Basie band.

This doesn't mean that certain standards of appraisal don't cut across all styles. As I outlined in the opening pages of this book, all jazz players, of any idiom, benefit from having a confident and supple sense of rhythm and tempo, an acute ear, an ability to move beyond clichés, control of tone, a distinctive musical personality, and so forth. You don't need to reinvent the listening experience with every new track. But an empathetic openness to the individual performers and their context and aspirations is essential. This is a matter of attitude, not musicology, and not much different from the way you ought to approach other life experiences. In every sphere of social interaction, that hermeneutic leap—that ability to put yourself in the mind frame of the other—is a virtue and a blessing. Jazz is no different.

I would like to stress one last attitudinal mandate, perhaps the most important, before concluding this chapter. I approach every new record, every performance, with optimism and (borrowing the words of lyricist Sammy Cahn) high hopes. I remember my earliest visits to jazz clubs when I was still a teenager. Before the music started, I would say to myself, "Almost anything could happen tonight. Almost anything!" Perhaps that sounds naïve, the breathless enthusing of a fan, not the sober reflections of a future critic and music historian, but I still can't imagine approaching jazz any other way. When I attend a classical concert, in contrast, I can tell by looking at the program exactly what I will hear. If it says Beethoven's Piano Sonata Number 8 (the *Pathétique*) is on the bill that evening, I can anticipate almost every note. Rock and pop concerts are a bit more unpredictable, but even in that setting I know the band will play its familiar hits and probably try to make them sound similar to the album, the proceedings 'enhanced' with stage props and visual effects, yet still essentially the same routines they did last night in a different city and will re-create at their next tour stop. But jazz, I learned at the very start of my exposure to it, plays by different rules. It is open to a much wider range of possibilities. The musicians themselves hardly know what they will play; the jazz world's fixation with improvisation ensures that strange and wonderful proceedings can unfold on the bandstand, perhaps during the very next song.

When I first encountered jazz critic Whitney Balliett's description of jazz as "the sound of surprise," I could only nod my head in agreement: he had captured in those four words exactly what drew me to this art form. And I can't help but believe that my openness to new sounds—openness is too gentle a word; let me call it my *craving* for new sounds—and experiences, this willingness to be surprised, has imparted an inexhaustible sensual pleasure to my vocation as critic. The late French literary critic Roland Barthes sometimes used the term *jouissance* to describe his personal response to his favorite texts, and the word, which lacks a precise equivalent in English, conveys a strange hybrid

sense of joy that possesses both sexual and aesthetic overtones. I want to encourage you to seek out this *jouissance*
of jazz.[11]

If you bring this attitude—combined with the listening skills described in the preceding pages—along on your
journey, you can move on to other artists not included in
the short list of innovators addressed in this chapter, and
feel confident that you are approaching them on the right
wavelength.

SEVEN

Listening to Jazz Today

ANY READER WHO HAS FOLLOWED ME TO THIS POINT MIGHT BE forgiven for assuming that learning about jazz is a matter of listening to recordings. After all, most of the musicians addressed in the preceding pages are no longer performing in concert. Unless jazz clubs start booking holograms, we've lost our chance to watch them on the bandstand. But I make no apologies for devoting so much attention to artists who no longer work the circuit or appear at the leading jazz festivals. A listener in the current day can't develop an informed sense of the art form without paying close attention to the legacies of Armstrong, Ellington, Coltrane, and the other past masters of the idiom. A sympathetic scrutiny of their music is still the best starting point for a study of this sort. And to do this, of course, we must turn to the body of recordings they left behind.

But we also need to remind ourselves that these innovators were working musicians, who performed night after
night in front of a constantly shifting audience, and that
digital tracks or grooves in vinyl only capture a small part
of what these artists created or embodied. The ideal way to
experience jazz will always be firsthand, at the source, fully
present at the moment of inspiration and realization. This
is probably true for all kinds of music, but especially so for
jazz, which places so much faith in spontaneity, in the belief
that each performance should aim at creating a unique and
irreplaceable epiphany for both artist and audience.

So this is the first reason you should care about jazz in
the present day: you can experience it the way the music
is meant to be experienced. In the flesh. As a ritual with its
own expectations and covenants. And as with any mean-
ingful ritual, the goal is not just to invoke the past but to
summon up powers of enchantment and transformation
and make them manifest in the present moment. This can't
really happen when listening to an old recording, or certainly not to the degree that you will encounter in live
performance. When I think back on all the great musical moments I have experienced, almost all of them happened at a nightclub or concert hall. Recordings have been
important to me too, and I probably have learned more
from them than from live events. But those special feelings,
that "immense elation and freedom, as the outlines of the
confining selfhood melt down"—forgive me for quoting
William James's *The Varieties of Religious Experience*, but he

comes closer to describing the spirit of a jazz performance than any music critic—only have been granted to me when in direct contact with musicians operating at peak creative levels. No record, however iconic, can deliver this. Only by immersing myself in jazz music of the current moment can I experience this. I suspect that the same will be true for you.[1]

I've heard jazz fans offer many reasons for why they don't attend live events. They sometimes protest that they prefer the older jazz styles. Or they cite the many limitations of current-day jazz musicians, who, in their opinion, lack some sort of vital spirit or soulfulness possessed by earlier generations of improvisers. Perhaps they want tunes that can serve as a mental soundtrack to noir 1950s fantasies, and only a West Coast jazz album from back in the day fits the bill. Or they enjoy the innocent exuberance of New Orleans traditional jazz, so they keep playing those old Satchmo tracks over and over. Or they want the jitterbugging beat of the big bands or the strident cacophony of free jazz at its most irreverent. I have no beef with such folks. Let all of them follow their own bliss and pick the tunes they want on that journey. But their arguments are unconvincing if used as justification for avoiding the current jazz scene. Let me emphasize my point by resorting to italics: *every jazz style described in this book is still alive and flourishing on the bandstand.*

In fact, the jazz world takes extreme measures to keep these sounds alive in concert. Not long ago, a jazz band re-created Miles Davis's *Kind of Blue* album note for note in its entirety. Yes, that's right, not just the solos but every drum hit and bass note was reenacted with scrupulous fidelity to the original. A few months later, Ravi Coltrane celebrated the fiftieth anniversary of his father's classic album *A Love Supreme* by performing the music live in concert. Almost at the same moment, a prominent jazz club hosted a Django Reinhardt music festival devoted to the pre–World War II gypsy guitar stylings of this historic performer. If your mood favors big bands, you can find almost every genus and species still playing for dancers. In fact, some classic Swing Era orchestras are still touring. You can hear the Glenn Miller and Count Basie bands even though their leaders left us long ago. The Duke Ellington band is still on the road, four decades after its leader's death. "The orchestra has never had a break since the 1920s," brags current-day conductor Charlie Young. "It's the oldest continuously performing jazz orchestra in history."[2] Stan Kenton, in contrast, stipulated in his will that no "ghost band" could continue after his death, but that hasn't prevented various alumni and tribute orchestras from bringing his music on the road. And if you are a fan of New Orleans and Chicago styles, you are especially fortunate. Hundreds, perhaps thousands, of trad jazz groups keep this music alive all over the world. I suspect that somebody somewhere is always playing "Tiger Rag" or "Basin Street Blues."

So even if you haven't updated your jazz tastes since Prohibition, this is no excuse to stay away from the current-day speakeasies and other venues where the music is still pouring out from the spigot.

But even better, open up your ears to jazz of the present moment.

Perhaps you have read articles about "the end of jazz" or other grand pronouncements about a state of crisis in the music. And if you believe these write-ups, you might conclude that jazz is to music what the Chicago Cubs are to baseball: a loser's bet and almost a symbol of futility. Most of these obituaries for an art form are shallow and unconvincing, but I don't entirely disagree with the doomsayers. From an *economic* standpoint, jazz is definitely suffering. The music is marginalized by mass media, and as a result jazz musicians almost never appear on television or radio or the homepage of *YouTube* and the other web-based arbiters of taste. Most mainstream periodicals ignore jazz and have for a long, long time. And on those rare occasions when they decide to cover it, they are constrained by the lack of expertise on their staff. The last jazz writer probably got laid off ten years ago, and the editors were raised on rock, pop, and hip-hop. Nothing wrong with that, but who can be surprised, given this state of affairs, when these same periodicals run flamboyant articles about the *death of jazz*? The editors are accurately representing the world they live in, a media-saturated environment in which jazz has been pushed to the sidelines to make room for the latest clickbait.

So we don't have good *metrics* in the jazz world. I accept it. But most of the things I love in life, starting with the

wife and kids and moving outward, don't have good metrics. Their value can't be reduced to dollars and cents, or
a ranking of what's trending in some target demographic.

On the other hand, if you judge jazz by the music itself—and the purpose of this entire book is to encourage
you in that attitude—and not as a cultural meme ranked
by clicks and views, you will reach a very different conclusion. The music is in great shape. The level of musicianship
is higher than ever. The range of sounds and styles wider
than ever. Every week I encounter something new and exciting on the jazz scene. And the music is more accessible
than ever before—I can even watch live, high-def video
streams of a jazz performance halfway around the world in
the comfort of my home. I can go to the club, or the club
will come to me! For a tiny subscription fee, I can enjoy a
wide range of new jazz recordings every week. That lux-
ury would have broken my budget during my student days,
when I sometimes had to choose between my jazz fix and
a hot meal. Good jazz is abundant, and this is well worth
celebrating.

But, of course, that abundance contributes to the perception of a crisis. There's just too much to choose from,
and outsiders to the music don't know where to begin. The
jazz narrative was much simpler fifty years ago, when we still
lived in the "heroic age" of the music. Back then, jazz fans
elevated one or two figures to a position of preeminence,
and it was easy to explain to the uninitiated where they
should focus their attention. When swing was the thing,

the critics told newbies to listen to Ellington, Goodman, and Basie. When bop was hot, hipsters turned squares onto Parker, Gillespie, and Monk. And so on. But what happens when we live in an age of diversity, when so many different ways of playing jazz flourish at the same time? What happens when *all the heroes are gone*? Or, put differently, when local heroes can be found everywhere around the globe? Even the most insightful critic is at a loss. You can't reduce the current jazz scene to two or three representative names. But is that a sign of decline, or an indication of vitality?

Let me make a plunge into the complexity, and try to sort it out. I could take the easy path, and just serve up a list of outstanding current-day jazz musicians. *Take these names, my friend; may they serve you well!* But I fear that I wouldn't be doing anyone any favors by such an approach. The eyes of the newcomer would glaze over, and the more knowledgeable fans would immediately start bickering about who was included and excluded on the list. So I absolutely refuse to give you that list.* What we need even more is to grasp the context in which these lists have meaning. So instead of reeling off a bunch of unfamiliar but very hip names, let me try to identify and decode the most powerful forces at work in jazz at the current moment. These forces are defining the ethos of the art form today. If you

---

*Okay, I give in. I provide in an appendix a list of the "elite 150" jazz artists in early or mid-career who deserve your attention. But don't jump to it right now, and don't take it too seriously. View it merely as a representative sample of outstanding current-day talent, not an exclusive club.

understand them, you will be better prepared to make sense of your next encounter with jazz, whether you're hanging out at the nightclub or plugged into your favorite hand-held device.

The first of these forces should come as no surprise to you, if only because it is probably already influencing every other aspect of your day-to-day life. I am talking about *globalization*. Yes, jazz is no different from your job, your mortgage, and the cost of gas at the pump. It responds to global forces, and even what happens on a local level gets inextricably connected with circumstances in far-flung places.

Not everyone benefits from these shifts. Those who previously were in a position of dominance face new competitive forces. For example, jazz festivals in Europe book fewer American artists nowadays. With so much home-grown talent—and every major city on the continent now boasts first-rate jazz bands—European promoters have less need to fly in expensive artists from New York and Los Angeles. The jazz scene in the Asia-Pacific region isn't quite as advanced, at least not at the present moment. But that is changing rapidly. These countries have been importing jazz from the United States for decades, but are starting to emerge as exporters of their best and brightest artists. We are witnessing a gradual leveling of the balance of musical trade. And this is more than just a matter of improving standards of musicianship among jazz players in these regions. Even more striking is the sense of confidence and self-determination I hear from these bands. When I lived overseas in my twenties, the jazz musicians I met were very focused on what the US performers were doing. They wanted to learn and imitate from the Americans, almost to the exclusion of other influences. But non-US jazz players have a different outlook today. When I travel now, the musicians are still knowledgeable about the American scene, but they increasingly want to talk about all the exciting jazz happening on their native soil. And they have plenty to talk about.

This makes my life as a jazz writer much more complicated than it was ten or twenty years ago. There is simply so much for me to follow, so much I could miss if I don't keep in touch with my peers around the globe and sift through lots of new music every week. But for the casual fan, this globalization is a blessing. Wherever you live, outstanding jazz is nearby. I couldn't have made that claim with so much assurance just a few years ago. But nowadays hot sounds are there for the taking, from Auckland to Zagreb. You may need to sniff around a bit to find them, because of the apparent media prohibition against covering current-day jazz, but they can't hide this stuff completely. And if you hear something really cool in an out-of-the-way place, tell me about it. Those of us in the subculture need to work together.

This globalization has contributed to the next major trend in the jazz world today: *hybridization*. Jazz techniques are getting applied in new ways, and almost every musical tradition in the world is getting mixed together with them. In some ways, this simply continues an old story. Jazz has always been more capable of digesting new musical ingredients than other genres. Even at its birth in New Orleans it was incorporating elements of the blues, marches, spirituals, and other sources of inspiration. But in the new global environment, this process of hybridization and expansion has been turbocharged. Nowadays, you will still hear jazz played on saxophones and trumpets, but also on the Japanese koto or Persian oud or Scottish bagpipe. You might encounter musicians performing an old jazz tune from the 1930s or trying their hand at jazzing up a grunge rock song or Indian raga. Multiethnic and multinational bands are increasingly the norm, especially in Europe, and the music is enriched and empowered by the diverse cultural backgrounds of the various participants. "We Are the World" would make for a lousy jazz song (although it was composed by a former jazz bassist), but it captures the ethos at work in the music, which is increasingly operating beyond the borders and boundaries that define the rest of our lives.

I believe that this is the most exciting development in music today, not just on the jazz scene, but in the world of aural culture generally. Yes, that's an extreme claim, but I stand behind it. I don't see how anyone can listen to these vibrant intersections of musical traditions—combinations of sounds that never previously coexisted, and each with thousands of years of legitimacy behind them—and not get jazzed by the results. Whenever I hear people of a certain age grumble that nothing new is happening in music, I have to shake my head in pity. They clearly aren't listening to the right stuff. And, yes, I must also admit to my delight in the extra-musical considerations involved in these trans-cultural collaborations. Perhaps we have failed to bridge the sociopolitical gulfs that separate all the peoples of the world, but at least on the bandstand we have shown both the possibility and the glorious upside from mutual respect, duty-free transactions, and non-coercive cooperation.

The third force sweeping through the jazz world to-day is *professionalization*. This doesn't mean that previous generations failed to take their craft seriously or aspire to the highest standards, but the new breed of jazz artist has trained and prepared in a very different way from the stars of yesteryear. The pioneers of jazz were mostly self-taught; they learned on the job and picked up what they could from fellow musicians along the way. The jazz performers of the twenty-first century, in contrast, have benefited from academic programs and professional training unavailable to their predecessors. Most of them have learned jazz in a sys-tematic, codified way in classroom settings and under the guidance of teachers with credentials in music instruction. They prepare for a jazz career the same way a future lawyer attends law school or an aspiring doctor attends medical school.

This marriage of jazz and academia is not without its downsides. You will hear scolding elders complain that the younger generation *lacks feeling*. Their playing is allegedly cold and clinical, just the kind of thing you would expect from someone who learned jazz out of a textbook. And, certainly, those who look to criticize the new crop of jazz talent can find examples to back up their generalizations. I do hear current-day jazz that sounds a bit too chilly, and perhaps this can be traced back to what's fashionable in jazz education. But I also encounter new jazz artists of the highest rank who have just as much fire and drive as the heroes of the past, and they are more expressive artists because of what they learned at school. My considered judgment is that these academic programs have done much more good than harm, and the balance is so tilted to the positive side that I wonder whether some ulterior motive doesn't distort the views of their critics. I can understand feeling a degree of envy—I spent twelve years in high school and various universities but never attended any institution that allowed me to learn jazz in a classroom. No courses in jazz harmony or jazz arranging or improvisation were offered. I had to learn on my own and in my own happenstance manner. I feel more than a tinge of regret that these options weren't available to me. But I can't blame those who now have these opportunities and seize them. Nor can I find anything negative in high schools and colleges embracing jazz and including it in their curriculums. Jazz has earned its place at the academic table.

How does this professionalization affect what you will hear in the jazz clubs today? Probably the best comparison is modern sports. The level of athleticism nowadays is unprecedented. Top-tier competitors jump higher, move faster, hit harder than ever before. In a track event, this improvement can even be quantified with a stopwatch or measuring stick. Of course, you can't measure these kinds of changes with the same exactitude in jazz, but I'm absolutely convinced that a similar process of improvement is at work. I can already hear those old-timers moaning and yelping at this claim, but it's simply true. Just check out the skill of the new millennium artist in playing unusual time signatures or complex song structures. People weren't performing "All the Things You Are" in 7/8 back in 1959—that magical year so prized by jazz nostalgists. And for a very good reason: the band would have fallen apart at the seams trying to pull it off. But now college students toss off this stuff at a blistering speed as if it's nothing.

The same is true of complex big band charts. This may sound like heresy, but if you listen closely enough to those classic jazz orchestral recordings featuring arranger Gil Evans and Miles Davis, the musicians are making mistakes. They weren't entirely comfortable with the music, and though the end result is sublime, you have to give the nod to today's players, who tackle far more complex scores with greater precision. When John Coltrane recorded "Giant Steps" back in the same era, the band was struggling to keep up—check out Tommy Flanagan's piano solo on that track and sympathize with his pain and suffering. But student jazz bands today play this piece without any perspiration. I recently heard a recording of an eleven-year-old who played "Giant Steps" like it was "Chopsticks." That's the world we live in. The evidence is irrefutable: jazz technical skills have advanced, no matter what you might have heard to the contrary.

For these reasons, I defend the youngsters, even though I sometimes encounter current-day players who have decided that assimilating the received wisdom of the past is an end in itself. But for the purposes of this book, I would prefer to put the burden of deciding this issue on your shoulders. Go listen to the music of a half dozen or so up-and-coming jazz bands filled with recent graduates of the best jazz conservatories, and make up your own mind. Are these young virtuosos world-beating hotshots or cold clinicians? If you listen long enough, you will encounter examples of both, and making these kinds of distinctions is at the heart of the listening experience in the jazz world today.

If you decide you want something more emotionally direct than an academically trained jazz band, you will be delighted by the last dominant trend on my list. Many of the leading record labels and younger jazz players are embarking on a project of artistic *rejuvenation*, driven by an ongoing dialogue with the leading commercial music styles of our day. This movement doesn't yet have a name. I often describe it as *Nu Jazz*, as do a few other observers of the scene, but I find that even experienced jazz cats look at me with a puzzled expression when I use that term. *Nu Jazz? What in the world are you talking about?* Others try to pigeonhole this music by lumping it together with previous movements to expand the jazz audience, such as jazz-rock fusion or smooth jazz. But that labeling misses most of what is fresh and new (nu?) in this work.

What exactly is Nu Jazz? It draws on the full range of sounds and tools on the contemporary music scene: loops and samples, raps and beats, electronica and remixes, R&B grooves and EDM vibes. The band might feature standard jazz instruments, but don't be surprised to see DJs and programmers participating too. More music might be coming out of the laptop at the side of the stage than from the horns in the front line. Or the live performance might just be the warm-up for the 'live' remix after the concert.

Jazz has always benefited from a dialogue with commercial music styles. This happened in New Orleans in 1900, and it's happening in jazz clubs today. This is the manifest destiny of jazz, an expansionary movement that never really ended. Jazz is like a frugal cook making ends meet—every leftover and stray ingredient gets thrown into the pot. Despite the stereotype of jazz musicians as snobs, the truth is the exact opposite—no practitioner in the current-day music world is more willing to draw on every possible source of inspiration. Even if commercial hit makers are (mostly) ignorant of what's going on in jazz, the jazz players are very aware of mainstream musical culture and won't hesitate to borrow from it to meet their own needs. This process can sometimes be awkward—I still cringe when I hear Miles Davis play "The Doo Bop Song" on his final studio album, the trumpeter who learned his craft alongside Charlie

Parker now deferring to less-than-inspired rapper Easy Mo Bee. And some of these projects are clearly sellouts, the jazz players more interested in the financial upside of crossover than the creative potential. But Davis himself proved, in other settings, that audience expansion and artistry can go hand in hand, and even a jazz legend can learn from whatever is buzzing on the current music scene. Put simply, the upside from these collaborations more than justifies the risks. Jazz musicians are invigorated by fresh sounds and new technological tools. Commercial artists gain in return by drawing on what jazz has to offer.

So I have made my attempt to simplify the extraordinary diversity and multiplicity of jazz today into these four themes: *globalization, hybridization, professionalization,* and *rejuvenation.* These trends are still unfolding, and with a degree of fluidity and unpredictability that suggests that they may still be in the early stages. Perhaps "trends" is a misleading term in this respect. These are more like inexorable forces that aren't likely to go "out of style" anytime soon. I suspect that these four forces will still shape the jazz idiom in exciting ways ten or twenty years from now.

Of course, this blueprint only hints at the riches you will encounter at the jazz club or concert. Even this brief survey of the current scene makes clear that jazz is hardly in the state of decline that some observers (usually those viewing it from a considerable distance) take so much relish in describing. Art forms that are stagnant or in actual decline don't show so much flux and change. They aren't quite so unpredictable. If jazz were like that, I could tell you with much more specificity what you would hear in live performance. If I were writing about opera, I could predict with 100 percent certainty that Puccini and Verdi will be coming to the opera house soon—and next year too, and the year after, and so on. Boogie woogie pianists are playing the same figures and progressions that their predecessors were using in the 1920s and will continue to do so next month, next year, next decade. If I were writing about polka, I could tell you to be on the lookout for an accordion; and if it's bluegrass, it will be a banjo, and so forth. That won't change anytime soon. Such assertions don't take much forecasting skill: some futures can be anticipated with pinpoint accuracy. But jazz isn't like that. Even as we consider the major forces at play in the current moment, we can hardly imagine which scenario for its future evolution is most likely. Like any living organism, jazz is still shaping its destiny.

Who is bold enough to put any limits on where the art form might go in the future? Certainly not me. As far as I can tell, audience members might soon be participating in the band's improvisations via their smartphone or some other handheld device. Or robots might step up to the bandstand and collaborate with the human performers. Maybe the process of improvisation applies to software as much as saxophony and can unfold in real time in ways we hardly grasp in the present moment with our hidebound views. Musicians might interact with each other via avatars.

Dead improvisers might rise again as digital constructs and take a solo on today's hits. With an art form so committed to spontaneity and risk taking, almost anything could happen. That fact may limit my skills as a prognosticator, but it is a great blessing for a fan of the jazz idiom in the twenty-first century.[3]

So this is my one certain prediction, irrefutable and rock solid, for your future as a jazz fan. Here it is: you will *not* be bored.

That's as safe a bet as I can make.

Which leads to my last bit of advice. I know that I have given a lot of it in the preceding pages, but I have one last nugget of wisdom to share. *Don't take my word for any of this.* Go out and hear for yourself. I've shared with you observations of a lifetime of listening to this music, but as the legal disclaimer always attests in these instances: your results may vary. I may have given you a recipe book, but the obligation is on your shoulders to do the cooking and tasting. And add some new dishes of your own. But that should be a pleasant responsibility.

Appendix

The Elite 150:
Early- and Mid-Career Jazz Masters

The intention here isn't to hand out honors but merely to suggest some current-day jazz artists worthy of your attention. So many potential fans stay away from today's jazz scene because they don't know where to start. They feel overwhelmed by too many names and tracks, gigs and playlists. By my estimate, around five thousand new jazz albums are released each year. Add to these around four hundred thousand commercial jazz recordings released during the last century. Even the experts struggle to keep up with all this music. So who can blame the casual fan for walking away from jazz, concluding that the music may be interesting, but it's hardly worth the effort? Others focus on a handful of historical figures, those acknowledged past masters whose works have stood the test of time. Why take a risk on a lesser-known young talent, they ask, when so many acknowledged innovators from the glory days can be studied and enjoyed?

I understand the reasoning of these fans but can't support it. You won't really experience the intensity and beauty of the jazz ethos unless you go into the clubs and concert halls, and discover what the music is like in the moment of creation. And the current-day talents are worthy of our support. The pioneers have left us, but we are blessed with many extraordinary jazz artists in our midst. Give them your attention and patronage. In return, they will broaden your musical perspectives and enrich your experiences as a listener.

This list, in alphabetical order, includes jazz artists in early and mid-career. I admire the elders of the genre, but those who have already enjoyed the biblical three score and ten years belong on a different list. The oldest artists on this list were born in the 1960s, and many of them are still in the early stages of their musical evolution. Most of them will still be shaping the jazz conversation for decades to come, and I want you to enjoy following the action.

Finally, let this list serve as a starting point in your investigation, not as an end point or closed system. I could easily have added another one hundred names, but it would be even better for you to move on to that stimulating exercise on your own. Happy listening!

The Elite 150 of
Early- and Mid-Career Jazz Masters

1. Rez Abbasi (guitar)
2. Jason Adasiewicz (vibraphone)
3. Cyrille Aimée (vocals)
4. Ambrose Akinmusire (trumpet)
5. Melissa Aldana (saxophone)
6. Ralph Alessi (trumpet)
7. Eric Alexander (saxophone)
8. Joey Alexander (piano)
9. JD Allen (saxophone)
10. Ben Allison (bass)
11. Darcy James Argue (composer)
12. Jeff Ballard (drums)
13. Nik Bärtsch (piano)
14. Django Bates (keyboards)
15. Brian Blade (drums)
16. Terence Blanchard (trumpet)
17. Theo Bleckmann (vocals)
18. Stefano Bollani (piano)
19. Kris Bowers (piano)
20. Till Brönner (trumpet)
21. Taylor Ho Bynum (cornet)
22. Francesco Cafiso (saxophone)
23. Joey Calderazzo (piano)
24. Ian Carey (trumpet)
25. Terri Lyne Carrington (drums)

26.   James Carter (saxophone)
27.   Regina Carter (violin)
28.   Chris Cheek (saxophone)
29.   Cyrus Chestnut (piano)
30.   Evan Christopher (clarinet)
31.   Gerald Clayton (piano)
32.   Anat Cohen (clarinet)
33.   Avishai Cohen (bass)
34.   Ravi Coltrane (saxophone)
35.   Sylvie Courvoisier (piano)
36.   Jamie Cullum (piano/vocals)
37.   Joey DeFrancesco (organ)
38.   Dave Douglas (trumpet)
39.   Mathias Eick (trumpet)
40.   Taylor Eigsti (piano)
41.   Kurt Elling (vocals)
42.   Orrin Evans (piano)
43.   Tia Fuller (saxophone)
44.   Jacob Garchik (trombone)
45.   Kenny Garrett (saxophone)
46.   Sara Gazarek (vocals)
47.   Robert Glasper (keyboards)
48.   Aaron Goldberg (piano)
49.   Wycliffe Gordon (trombone)
50.   Larry Grenadier (bass)
51.   Mats Gustafsson (saxophone)
52.   Wolfgang Haffner (drums)
53.   Mary Halvorson (guitar)

54. Craig Handy (saxophone)
55. Roy Hargrove (trumpet)
56. Eric Harland (drums)
57. Stefon Harris (vibraphone)
58. Miho Hazama (composer)
59. Arve Henriksen (trumpet)
60. Vincent Herring (saxophone)
61. John Hollenbeck (drummer)
62. Susie Ibarra (percussion)
63. Jon Irabagon (saxophone)
64. Ethan Iverson (piano)
65. Vijay Iyer (piano)
66. Christine Jensen (saxophone)
67. Ingrid Jensen (trumpet)
68. Norah Jones (vocals)
69. Ryan Keberle (trombone)
70. Grace Kelly (saxophone)
71. Guillermo Klein (piano)
72. Julian Lage (guitar)
73. Biréli Lagrène (guitar)
74. Steve Lehman (saxophone)
75. David Linx (vocals)
76. Lionel Loueke (guitar)
77. Rudresh Mahanthappa (saxophone)
78. Tony Malaby (saxophone)
79. Mat Maneri (violin)
80. Grégoire Maret (harmonica)
81. Branford Marsalis (saxophone)

82. Wynton Marsalis (trumpet)
83. Christian McBride (bass)
84. Donny McCaslin (saxophone)
85. John Medeski (keyboards)
86. Brad Mehldau (piano)
87. Vince Mendoza (composer)
88. Nicole Mitchell (flute)
89. Robert Mitchell (piano)
90. Ben Monder (guitar)
91. Jason Moran (piano)
92. Youn Sun Nah (vocals)
93. Qasim Naqvi (drummer)
94. Fabiano do Nascimento (guitar)
95. Vadim Neselovskyi (piano)
96. Arturo O'Farrill (piano)
97. Linda Oh (bass)
98. Greg Osby (saxophone)
99. Gretchen Parlato (vocals)
100. Nicholas Payton (trumpet)
101. Jeremy Pelt (trumpet)
102. Danilo Pérez (piano)
103. Jean-Michel Pilc (piano)
104. Gregory Porter (vocals)
105. Chris Potter (saxophone)
106. Noah Preminger (saxophone)
107. Dafnis Prieto (drums)
108. Joshua Redman (saxophone)
109. Eric Reed (piano)

110. Tomeka Reid (cello)
111. Ilja Reijngoud (trombone)
112. Marcus Roberts (piano)
113. Matana Roberts (saxophone)
114. Joris Roelofs (saxophone)
115. Kurt Rosenwinkel (guitar)
116. Florian Ross (piano)
117. Gonzalo Rubalcaba (piano)
118. Cécile McLorin Salvant (vocals)
119. Antonio Sánchez (drummer)
120. Jenny Scheinman (violin)
121. Maria Schneider (composer)
122. Christian Scott (trumpet)
123. Ian Shaw (vocals)
124. Jaleel Shaw (saxophone)
125. Yeahwon Shin (vocals)
126. Matthew Shipp (piano)
127. Solveig Slettahjell (vocals)
128. Omar Sosa (piano)
129. Luciana Souza (vocals)
130. Esperanza Spalding (bass/voice)
131. Becca Stevens (vocals)
132. Loren Stillman (saxophone)
133. Marcus Strickland (saxophone)
134. Helen Sung (piano)
135. Craig Taborn (keyboards)
136. Dan Tepfer (piano)
137. Jacky Terrasson (piano)

138.   Thundercat (bass)
139.   Ryan Truesdell (composer)
140.   Mark Turner (saxophone)
141.   Hiromi Uehara (piano)
142.   Gary Versace (keyboards)
143.   Cuong Vu (trumpet)
144.   Joanna Wallfisch (vocals)
145.   Kamasi Washington (saxophone)
146.   Marcin Wasilewski (piano)
147.   Bugge Wesseltoft (piano)
148.   Anthony Wilson (guitar)
149.   Warren Wolf (vibraphone)
150.   Miguel Zenón (alto sax)

Acknowledgments

I want to thank everyone who helped me in my own journey as a musician and writer. I must start the list with my uncle Ted, who died in a plane crash a few months before I was born but left behind a piano in my parents' home. If he had lived beyond the tender age of twenty-eight, he would have been the music scholar in the family and perhaps a well-known composer too. As it stands, I inherited his name and spent many happy hours at his keyboard. That was the start of my own love affair with music.

I later learned from teachers, mentors, friends, and fellow musicians. I could never do an adequate job of listing their names or explaining how much they broadened my perspectives and fired my imagination. But I want to express my deepest gratitude to all of them and to everyone who nurtures the talents of youngsters, whether in music or any other field of endeavor.

I can do a better job of listing those who helped in the actual preparation of this book. These generous and talented individuals read parts of the manuscript and gave me

invaluable input. Let me thank Bob Belden, Darius Brubeck, Steve Carlton, Dan Cavanagh, Roanna Forman, Bill
Kirchner, Mark Lomanno, Stuart Nicholson, John O'Neill,
Lewis Porter, Zan Stewart, Mark Stryker, Dan Tepfer, Scott
Timberg, and Denny Zeitlin. Their involvement doesn't
imply endorsement of the views presented in these pages,
and I especially want to absolve them from responsibility
for any of the limitations of this book. But the finished
work is much better because of them.

I want to acknowledge the catalytic role of Katy
O'Donnell, who was extremely helpful in the early stages
of this project. I owe a huge debt to Lara Heimert, my
editor, and to all her colleagues who have helped make
this book a reality. I am also indebted to Roger Labrie and
Beth Wright, whose comments on the manuscript proved
invaluable in the final stages of writing and editing. Finally
I want to share publicly the gratitude that I express pri-
vately every day to my wife, Tara, and our sons, Michael
and Thomas. As Duke Ellington—who opens and closes
this book—often said, *I love you madly!*

Notes

Introduction

1. The story may be apocryphal. This scornful rejoinder is usually assigned to Fats Waller, but sometimes credited to other jazz figures, with everyone from Louis Armstrong to Stan Kenton alleged to have said it—invariably in response to a "sweet old lady" who asks: "What is jazz?" The zeal with which jazz experts repeat this 'definition' of jazz over and over again is revealing. Marshall Stearns, the godfather of jazz academia, even relied on it for the opening sentence of his magisterial *The Story of Jazz* (New York: Oxford University Press, 1956), 3.

One: The Mystery of Rhythm

1. John Miller Chernoff, *African Rhythm and African Sensibility* (Chicago: University of Chicago Press, 1979), 54.

2. I summarize some of the more interesting research on the physiological impact of rhythm in my book *Healing Songs* (Durham, NC: Duke University Press, 2006), see esp. 60–65, 162–167.

3. Ted Gioia and Fernando Benadon, "How Hooker Found His Boogie: A Rhythmic Analysis of a Classic Groove," *Popular Music* 28, no. 1 (2009): 19–32.

Two: Getting Inside the Music

1. Quoted in Whitney Balliett's essay "Le Grand Bechet" in *Jelly Roll, Jabbo and Fats: 19 Portraits in Jazz* (New York: Oxford University Press, 1984), 37.

2. Zan Stewart, email to author, May 21, 2015.

3. Edgar Wind, *Art and Anarchy* (New York: Knopf, 1963), 28.

4. Michael Ullman, *Jazz Lives: Portraits in Words and Pictures* (Washington, DC: New Republic Books, 1980), 229.

Three: The Structure of Jazz

1. Paul Bowles, "Duke Ellington in Recital for Russian War Relief," *New York Herald-Tribune*, January 25, 1943, 12–13, reprinted in *The Duke Ellington Reader*, ed. Mark Tucker (New York: Oxford University Press, 1993), 165–166.

Four: The Origins of Jazz

1. Ted Gioia, *Love Songs: The Hidden History* (New York: Oxford University Press, 2015), 92–120.

2. Thomas Brothers, *Louis Armstrong's New Orleans* (New York: Norton, 2006), 239.

3. Alan Lomax, *Mister Jelly Roll* (New York: Duell, Sloan & Pearce, 1950), 271. Most books refer to the singer as Mamie Desdoumes, drawing on Lomax's spelling, but census documents make clear that her name was Desdunes. Parish records tracked down by researcher Peter Hanley suggest that this Creole woman, who ranks among the earliest known blues performers, was born in New Orleans in 1879.

4. Quote from Papa John Joseph cited in John McCusker, *Creole Trombone: Kid Ory and the Early Years of Jazz* (Jackson: University Press of Mississippi, 2012), 54. Other comments on Bolden are cited in Donald Marquis, *In Search of Buddy Bolden: First Man of Jazz* (Baton Rouge: Louisiana State University Press, 1978), 105, 111, 197.

Five: The Evolution of Jazz Styles

1. Ernest J. Hopkins, "In Praise of 'Jazz,' a Futurist Word Which Has Just Joined the Language," *San Francisco Bulletin*, April 5, 1913, reprinted in Lewis Porter, *Jazz: A Century of Change* (New York: Schirmer, 1999), 6–8.

2. Nat Hentoff and Nat Shapiro, *Hear Me Talkin' to Ya* (New York: Rinehart, 1955), 142–143.

3. Duke Ellington, *Music Is My Mistress* (Garden City, NY: Doubleday, 1973), 92.

4. Gary Giddins, "Cecil Taylor: An American Master Brings the Voodoo Home," *Village Voice*, April 28, 1975, 125.

5. I note that Googling "Marsalis" + "jazz" + "controversy" brings back links to about a hundred thousand web pages. But that is a subject for a different book.

Six: A Closer Look at Some Jazz Innovators

1. Michael Segell, *The Devil's Horn: The Story of the Saxophone, from Noisy Novelty to King of Cool* (New York: Picador, 2005), 283.

2. Sonny Rollins as told to Marc Myers, "Transformed, 'Body and Soul,'" *Wall Street Journal*, May 9, 2014.

3. John Chilton, *The Song of the Hawk* (Ann Arbor: University of Michigan Press, 1990), 303.

4. Duke Ellington, *Music Is My Mistress* (Garden City, NY: Doubleday, 1973), 446. Ellington's comment to Ralph Gleason comes from the pilot episode of Gleason's *Jazz Casuals* television show, taped at the KQED studio on July 10, 1960.

5. "Billy Strayhorn Interview by Bill Coss (1962)," in *The Duke Ellington Reader*, edited by Mark Tucker (New York: Oxford University Press, 1993), 502. Duke Ellington, *Music Is My Mistress* (Garden City, NY: Doubleday, 1973), 446.

6. Previn made this comment to critic Ralph Gleason. See Ralph Gleason, *Celebrating the Duke and Louis, Bessie, Billie, Bird, Carmen, Miles, Dizzy, and Other Heroes* (Boston: Little, Brown, 1975), 168. Stan Kenton led a popular and ambitiously experimental jazz big band from the early 1940s through the late 1970s.

7. John S. Clarkeson, president and chief executive officer of the Boston Consulting Group at the time, elaborates on this aspect of Ellington's skill

set in the pamphlet "Jazz vs. Symphony," *Boston Consulting Group Perspectives* (Boston: Boston Consulting Group, 1990).

8. Billie Holiday with William Dufty, *Lady Sings the Blues: The 50th Anniversary Edition* (New York: Broadway Books, 2006), 3.

9. Mihaly Csikszentmihalyi, *Flow: The Psychology of Optimal Experience* (New York: Harper and Row, 1990). No book on psychology has more to offer students and practitioners of the jazz idiom than *Flow*, and its teachings are by no means limited to music.

10. Joe Goldberg, *Jazz Masters of the 50s* (New York: Macmillan, 1965), 231. Davis later softened his stance on Coleman, and you can even hear the latter's influence on *Miles Smiles* (1967).

11. Whitney Balliett, *The Sound of Surprise: 46 Pieces on Jazz* (New York: Dutton, 1959). Roland Barthes, *The Pleasure of the Text*, translated by Richard Miller (New York: Hill and Wang, 1975).

Seven: Listening to Jazz Today

1. William James, *The Varieties of Religious Experience: A Study in Human Nature*, edited by Eugene Taylor and Jeremy Carrette (New York: Routledge, 2002), 213.

2. Randall G. Mielke, "After 92 Years, Duke Ellington Orchestra Still Offers Surprises," *Chicago Tribune*, September 3, 2015.

3. In fact, all of these futuristic approaches to jazz are taking place, to some degree, in the present day. See, for example, Charles Q. Choi, "Jazz-Playing Robots Will Explore Human-Computer Relations," *Scientific American*, October 22, 2015; Andrew R. Chow, "Billie Holiday, via Hologram, Returning to the Apollo," *New York Times*, September 9, 2015; and Oliver Hödl, Fares Kayali, and Geraldine Fitzpatrick, "Designing Interactive Audience Participation Using Smart Phones in a Musical Performance," research paper presented at the 2014 International Computer Music Conference in Ljubljana, Slovenia.

Index

Ted Gioia is a jazz pianist, an award–winning music historian, and the author of ten books, including *The History of Jazz* and *The Jazz Standards*. He previously served on the faculty of Stanford University's Department of Music. Gioia is currently a columnist for *The Daily Beast* and writes regularly on music, books, and popular culture.

Photograph courtesy of Dave Shafer